Education for Freedom

Education for Freedom

HAROLD M. SCHRODER
Princeton University

MARVIN KARLINS
City University of New York

JACQUELINE O. PHARES
Princeton University

John Wiley & Sons, Inc.
New York London Sydney Toronto

Library of Congress Cataloging in Publication Data:

Schroder, Harold M
    Education for freedom

    Includes bibliographical references.
      1. Education—Aims and objectives. 2. Liberty.
I. Karlins, Marvin, joint author. II. Phares,
Jacqueline O., joint author. III. Title.

LB1025.2.S36   370.11   72-8808
ISBN O-471-76330-6

Printed in the United States of America

10 9 8 7 6 5 4 3 2 1

Dedications from the authors:

To Molly, Jeannie and Libby
H. M. S.
To Jim and Diane
M. K.
To Tony, Jamie and Woody
J. O. P.

"Civilization is a race between education and catastrophe."

H. G. Wells

Preface

Today there is growing concern among citizens of all ages that our educational system has failed to give students the skills they need to face the new and challenging problems of our rapidly changing society. There is an uneasy feeling that our pedagogical practices—from kindergarten through graduate school—have not prepared us to win the race against catastrophe. The signs attesting to our poor performance in this race are everywhere: the alienated student; the increasing gap between the objectives of educational institutions and the needs of society; and our simplistic thinking about social issues and our callous disregard for our fellowman.

Our argument is that the major weakness of contemporary education in the United States is its inability to prepare twentieth-century youth for the challenges and obligations of twentieth-century democracy; our children are not learning the skills necessary to be adaptive and innovative in a political system that stimulates change and requires individual initiative.

If our democratic form of government is to survive and prosper in this new age, American education must prepare our children to deal with freedom. It can accomplish this goal by teaching our youth *how to think,* a capacity not to be confused with the amount of knowledge a student acquires. The ability to think—to cope with problems, to seek information and uncertainty, and to process information in new and meaningful ways—is learned. The development of this creative ability, therefore, cannot be left to chance. It must become a primary goal of education in a new problem-oriented, interdisciplinary pedagogical environment. Increasing the complexity and maturity of thinking prepares a child to meet the requirements he will face in future life; it gives him the skills he will need to deal effectively with the problems and obligations posed by our pluralistic, open form of government.

Children are not born free. They learn freedom, and the lessons are not easy—particularly in today's world. Yet, we believe that freedom as *a way of thought* must precede freedom as a way of life. The way that one goes about attaining this freedom is the main topic of this book.

This book was written while the authors were at Princeton University. Presently, Dr. Schroder is Director of the Problem Laboratory Program at Southern Illinois University (Edwardsville), Dr. Karlins is an Associate Professor of Psychology at the City College at the City University of New York, and Ms. Jacqueline Phares is engaged in research in Princeton, New Jersey where she just served as Director of Research for the New Jersey Delegation to the White House Conferences on Children and Youth.

Harold M. Schroder   Marvin Karlins   Jacqueline O. Phares

Acknowledgments

The authors would like to thank H. P. Cole for his careful and critical reading of the manuscript. His suggestions were of great value in all stages of writing this book. Also, our thanks to Joe Jordan, our editor at John Wiley. His help and encouragement throughout this undertaking was greatly appreciated.

H. M. S.
M. K.
J. O. P.

Contents

Education for Freedom

"Democracies collapse only when they fail to use intelligent, imaginative methods for solving problems. The kind of citizen here called for is a far cry from the model of a quiz program champion of a few years ago, and he is also more than a 'well rounded individual'. . . ."

E. P. Torrance

1. Educational Goals and Citizenship

This book is based on several assumptions. The first is our belief that the basic goal of education in a free society is to prepare a child to meet the requirements he will face in future life. The second is that a democratic society will remain democratic only to the extent that its citizens are trained to deal effectively with the problems and obligations posed by a pluralistic, open form of government. Third, we postulate that our world today is marked by an ever-accelerating rate of change and an ever-increasing complexity in both technology and human organization, and that this change and complexity pose the greatest problem, as well as the greatest challenge, which our democracy faces.

Since the middle of this century, we have lived amidst an explosion of scientific and technological breakthroughs. Under such conditions, knowledge is often outmoded before the student can begin to use it. Nor can we be sure what skills will be needed in the future. Education is no longer relevant to the changes perceived by our youth. In the face of such forward thrusts, society appears to be coming apart. It is as if there were no overall purpose holding us together. We experience failure and frustration in relating to each other: family solidarity is crumbling; relationships between ethnic groups are changing and strained; criminal acts are increasing; and the gaps between the productive and unproductive, the rich and the poor, the urban and the suburban are widening.

CONFRONTING THE CHALLENGE OF CHANGE

If, indeed, change—constant, accelerating, ubiquitous—is the most striking characteristic of the world we live in, we must train citizens who are not frightened by change and its constant companions, uncertainty and complexity. We must produce citizens who can, in Jerome Bruner's words, "cope" with the change and complexity rather than "defend" against them. We must redefine ability, self, citizenship, and identity to be relevant to the new world. Should we fail, the psychological crisis will worsen. The symptoms present today—individual feelings of meaninglessness, lack of pride, intergroup and interpersonal aggression, growing bureaucracy, the widening hiatus between the privileged and underprivileged, the deteriorating quality of life—will continue unabated. Social order and individual constraints will gradually erode with a citizenry ill-prepared to deal with the complexities of a constantly changing environment. A more autocratic, authoritarian regime will begin to emerge as democratic man seeks an escape from freedom, and our open society will slowly expire.

American education, therefore, must prepare our children to deal with freedom. As J. W. Gardner says, "we must equip them to understand and cope with change . . . we must give them the critical qualities of mind and the durable qualities of character which will serve them in circumstances we cannot now even predict. It is not just technical competence which is needed. A society such as ours is dependent upon . . . many kinds of complex understanding. It requires large numbers of individuals with depth of judgment, perspectives and broad comprehension of the problems facing our world." We must teach our children to utilize freedom of thought and individual initiative in the service of man. We must teach them to be innovative and flexible in a world of flux and uncertainty. Teaching children *how* to be free—giving them the ability to create and to adapt—might well be the most awesome and pressing task facing America as we approach the year 2000. It is the task of this book.

But, one might well question at this point, isn't contemporary American education teaching children to be free? No. It is our passionate contention that, despite the lip service paid to this goal every graduation day, our school environments and our pedagogical practices are *not* producing free men; and it is this failure that is at the core of many of our sociopolitical problems. Much of the reason for this failure can be understood if we examine the background and premises on which our current educational practices rest.

THE BACKGROUND TO OUR CURRENT EDUCATIONAL CRISIS

Our contemporary educational practices were developed when the world was far more static than it is today; man, society, and knowledge moved at a more leisurely pace. Change was more gradual; adjustment more simple. The skills and rules (be they science, civics, mathematics, or whatever) which a child learned were, for the most part, quite relevant to the conditions he would face in future life. There were changes in the conditions, certainly, and some of the school practices were modified accordingly, but the changes were relatively minor, and the modifications were often via short term, specific training programs. Even when cultural change made educational change mandatory, the modifications were often delayed (with little consequence) until the next generation came along.

Under such conditions, parallel and fitting psychological theories of learning emerged (e.g., Thorndike, Skinner, Hull). These theories were not only accepted in rarified academic circles but, more importantly, served to influence educational practices in this country. Despite their subtle differences, these theories shared an important basic assumption about education: learning can be effectively achieved when an agent (parent, teacher, machine) uses external rewards and punishments to shape and control the child's behavior. Using this theoretical orientation, scientists and educators spent a great deal of time finding out ways to enhance the rapid acquisition of desired behaviors, knowledge, and rules.

All of this might have remained of interest only to the student of psychological literature if such theories had not had the impact they did in shaping the criterion or aim of American education. That criterion became, quite simply, the amount of knowledge a student could acquire and/or the level of performance he could attain. Furthermore, the measurement of how well this aim was achieved was measured by tests and expressed as grades. This criterion or aim of American education remains basically unchanged today. Note that the emphasis here is upon "what" and "how much" a person learns; it is what we call *"content learning."* Thus, educational development in our country is defined as content learning, and grades and tests (including intelligence tests) have become the metric or standard against which different methods of education are evaluated.

Content learning has valuable aspects, certainly, but it is our contention that such an orientation, by itself, is not enough in our contemporary world of catapulting change. The traditional educational and teaching practices— developed in a more placid era—are unable to provide the emerging adult with the orientation, skills, and adaptability he must have to survive meaningfully in our kaleidoscopic age. Traditional content teaching procedures are unable to keep pace with the revolutionary learning requirements of today's student. As Carl Rogers has pointed out, "Probably the greatest single social problem of this century . . . is the question 'how rapidly can the human organism adapt to change' . . . Can human organisms absorb and assimilate such tremendous amounts of change? Certainly not by adhering to the static knowledge and static guidelines which have been the hallmarks of education, religion, and culture for many centuries. It can only be through adopting a *process* mode of living, finding a security in the *process* of change, rather than in the fixity of knowledge, belief, or conviction, that man can survive in this incredibly changing world."

We cannot return to a simpler, quieter world. Nor can we continue to use the educational philosophies which grew out of that quieter world. We must accept and apply a new theory of education and development that will, if put into practice, provide our citizens with the ability to benefit from freedom in our turbulent times.

THE NEED FOR PROCESS-CENTERED EDUCATION

How does one go about educating a child in the ways of freedom? By developing an educational program that includes *process* as well as *content* goals in the classroom. We will suggest that the traditional methods of American educators are almost exclusively concerned with *what* people think (content goals) rather than *how* they think (process goals). This emphasis is reflected in contemporary educational measurement that focuses on the amount of information a student has acquired or the performances he has mastered. Process goals—the way we learn to think or process information—are largely ignored, both in emphasis and measurement. In many ways, this stress on content goals has led us to view the student as a computer—with academic excellence being determined by the amount of information a pupil can "store" and recall at a given time.

Educational practice based on content goals can admirably prepare a student to overcome static and defined problems in a relatively stable environment. But, we will argue, education based on content goals is inadequate for students who must contend with novel and unexpected contingencies in a rapidly changing world. It is in this environment of flux and uncertainty (which, we claim, describes twentieth century America) that process goals become relevant.

The basic challenge today, for a free society, is not simply "knowledge" alone; what is "known," as we have seen, changes. The challenge, the necessity, is "discovery"; it is to cultivate in each future citizen the ability to generate new information, to discover and make use of new relationships, and to be flexible and adaptive. In short, we must emphasize the *process* goals of learning—"how" a child thinks; "how" content is learned; the necessity of seeking out information and putting it together in new and meaningful ways. We must be concerned not only with how much information is known, but how that information is utilized in dealing with the unknown; we must learn to judge a student not only by the amount of information he has accumulated and can recall but also by how effectively he can utilize information at his disposal in coping with his world. The focus must be on what we call *"information processing"* (Schroder et al, 1967; Karlins, 1968; Schroder, 1970), the process by which information is learned. The distinction between content and process learning is important. In school and at home, in the history class and the science laboratory, in the classroom and on the playground, the child is not only learning specific skills and information—he is also learning ways to process that information, ways of thinking about and relating to the world.

Are process goals feasible? From a scientific point of view, there is a growing body of evidence to indicate that they are. It has already been shown that under certain developmental conditions or in certain educational environments, children develop: (1) an *intrinsic* interest in their own and others' performance; (2) a readiness to experience change in social or technological situations accompanied by a spirit of discovering; (3) an ability to fully understand and respect the points of view of others; (4) a problem solving strategy in which these diverse and conflicting perspectives become the foundation on which decisions are made; and (5) the ability to simultaneously stand alone and to pose questions that require the mutual participation of others for there solution (Piaget, 1952; Hunt, J., 1966; Bruner, 1960; Biggs, 1968; Moore and Anderson, 1967; Schroder, et al., 1967; Cole, 1970).

From reading the above list, the reader might be aware of a "spin off" benefit to be gained through process learning: such cognitive training does more than prepare the individual for coping with a complex world; it also makes him more tolerant and interested in others. (We will argue in a later chapter that process education might help relieve some of our social-political problems, such as racial prejudice.) Through process learning, it might be possible to produce a generation of students who respect the rights, opinions, and basic freedoms of others. In this sense, the distinction between learning and citizenship is not only artificial, but false. At home and in school the child is not only learning skills and information, he is, at the same time, learning ways to process information. We will argue that the person who is able to process information in complex ways will be a better citizen, both in his capacity to live creatively and in interpersonal harmony. It is the task of education to give each American child the information processing skills he will need to face his world and his neighbors.

It is important, however, that we be able to measure these process goals and outcomes. The report card must be changed so that it now tells us about *how* a child thinks (process goals) as well as *what* he thinks (content goals). We must be able to judge progress in information processing as well as in information acquisition. We shall pay considerable attention to the measurement question in this book because, if there are no means to assess the growth of information-processing ability, the older criteria will persist, and no educational program devoted to process goals can be possible.

SUMMARY

We live today in a world marked by accelerating technological and social change, by increasing complexity and uncertainty. In such an environment, educational procedures developed during the era of relative stability and certainty are no longer able to provide the student with the skills he needs to exist effectively in contemporary society. It is suggested that an emphasis on *process* goals rather than exclusively on *content* goals of education—*how* people use the information they are taught—might better prepare the individual to live creatively in his world and harmoniously with his fellowman.

"It is still sad but true that the greatest instructional fallacy of mother and child, teacher and student, is the notion of telling as learning."

E. M. Bowers and W. G. Hollister

2. Education as Content Learning

METHODOLOGY AND GOALS

Content learning is the traditional educational philosophy and methodology used almost exclusively in schools and universities (and in many homes) today. It has a time-honored tradition behind it in western civilization, with certain notable exceptions such as Socrates. As the label indicates, the central concern of the training agent (parent, teacher, machine) in this approach is focused on the content that the child is expected to learn or know —the facts, sequences of events, generalizations, solutions, etc. The fundamentals of the methodology are quite simple. There are variations on the theme—lockstep, team teaching, egg-crate, sequential curriculum—but the fundamentals remain the same. That is, the agent gives the information, the concepts, the codes, the solutions via lecture, assigned readings, syllabi, etc., to the student. This information is to be stored in memory and retrieved when the agent presents the appropriate signal (direct questioning or posing a problem that requires the learned-memorized content for its solution).

In this view of education and child training, *mastery of content,* whether it be English, mathematics, social manners, or religion, *becomes the standard* or criterion by which development is defined and measured. In the preschool years, for instance, a child's developmental level—his "readiness" to be able to "learn" more—is measured or indicated by such content-laden or "knowledge" variables as his habits of cleanliness and neatness, his ability to follow rules, to remember names of people and places, to know or recognize words, numbers, and so on. For example, parents judge the progress of their children who regularly watch "Sesame Street" by how well the child can count up to twenty or can recognize certain words or letters of the alphabet.

Once the formal school years begin, the emphasis upon acquiring and memorizing content intensifies. One of the central aims of formal education, from this viewpoint, is to increase the amount of knowledge acquired and to raise the level of performance achieved in whatever the particular content or "subject" area may be. The level or criterion of the child's development, that is, the amount of information he has stored and the "quality" of his performance, is expressed as a "grade." Furthermore, his potential ability to achieve a high grade is often assessed by a content-oriented instrument— the IQ test.[1] This "grade" criterion of performance is quite useful in assessing the amount of information or knowledge that has been acquired via the traditional training methods. And, certainly, this kind of training—mastery of content—can be very effective in producing a high performance level. The child often does learn the information he is expected to learn and often learns it rapidly and effectively.

So far we have talked about the emphasis on content in the traditional approach to education. There is another characteristic of this approach: it is *agent* (teacher, parent, machine) *oriented.* In the content-learning method of education, the teacher (or parent or machine) acts as a storehouse of information—a repository of concepts, rules, or units of knowledge that he selectively transmits to the child. The child, in turn, is expected to learn what the training agent teaches so that he may use such material at a later time. In this system of education, the agent-child relationship is analogous to that of a doctor to his patient or a programmer to a computer. The child, like the patient or computer, is a passive recipient of information transmitted by the training agent; that is, it is "fed into him" and acted upon in a spirit of rote compliance.

In an agent-oriented approach, the environment is quite *external* to the learner. The material to be mastered comes prepackaged and from outside; the solutions or answers (correct responses) are given from outside as are the reinforcements: rewards for the correct response and punishments for the wrong one. Learning is "the passive reception of someone else's story" (Postman and Weingartner, 1969). All of which means that the child is learning something more in this kind of environment than just the particular subject matters at hand, be they trigonometry or how to negotiate a set of stair-steps. We shall discuss that "something more" a bit later on since it has profound implications for both the cognitive and personality development of the child.

It is this *content-centered, agent-oriented* educational method that is used almost without exception at all levels of education in the United States, and many of the physical and other aspects of school or university design and functioning follow accordingly. The teacher, wittingly or unwittingly, is forced into an omnipotent role since he is the repository of the knowledge that is to be imparted to the students. And so the classroom is designed with the teacher and his desk at the head, and rows of little desks occupied by groups of children who receive ready-packaged bits of knowledge usually in the form of books. Thus books become the technology of the school and educational practice is dominated by books. The packages are used according to the trainer's instructions, and the answers (responses) of the child are either rewarded or punished by the external source.

This external source does not always have to be the teacher himself. In the past few years we have witnessed a dazzling array of techniques, innovations, and devices usually labeled as "self-teaching" or "programmed learning" and ranging from closed-circuit TV to teaching machines to workbooks designed as teaching machines. Many parents and educators have welcomed their appearance in the hope or belief that they signaled a true breakthrough in the traditional educational methodology. Others have feared that they herald a kind of dehumanized, Orwellian school of the future. The point of the matter, however, is that all of these innovations or "improvements" are merely refinements of the same content-oriented approach. They are useful. They are effective. They do, for the most part, instill knowledge (definitions, names, etc.) rapidly and efficiently into the child's head. But they are not departures from the content-learning syndrome; the emphasis is still upon "knowing" or learning a certain number of things, and the instructional environment is still agent-oriented and external to the learner. The student is still expected to be the compliant recipient of someone else's answers to someone else's questions, with the same reinforcements externally applied (although in the case of programmed learning, the reward or punishment may have the advantage of not being publicly announced before a class of one's peers).

Perhaps the most telling impact of content-based, agent-oriented education is experienced by the student in the classroom lecture situation. Here, the teacher becomes a "deity at the podium," dispensing neatly packaged units of information to captive students stitting in classrooms designed for mass learning and mass audiences. Such a teaching approach is often characterized by:

1. *A fixed teaching pattern.* There is little, if any, deviation from a set lesson plan; the result being the student has little to say about what is taught, how it is taught and, in some cases, the rate at which it is taught.

2. *Emphasis on passive learning.* It is seldom that a student is rewarded for actively questioning and challenging what he is being taught. He is expected

in many ways to function in a "sponge-like" manner: soaking up the information presented and wringing it out on an exam or term paper. In such an atmosphere, the pupil often comes to regard information as a set of "givens" —a series of facts or solutions not open to dispute. The development of a healthy skepticism for what is said—the willingness to challenge and examine subject matter—certainly does not flourish in such circumstances. This is not surprising. Many educational environments geared to content learning are rigid, stable, and unresponsive to attempted student manipulation. It is often easier for the learner to agree with what is said than to dispute its merit: how easy is it, for example, for a student to challenge a professor's opinion before 150 fellow students during a 50 minute lecture?

3. *Little (if any) student-teacher interaction.* The student is often denied the opportunity to interact with the training agent, to carry on a dialogue about what he is learning. Such interaction is sometimes impossible in classes taught by closed circuit or educational TV. Under these conditions, the "feedback" problem is acute: during the broadcast the instructor has no way of knowing whether his students understand the lesson and the students have no way of questioning the teacher about the lecture.

As we have already stated, whatever the variations or combinations of the traditional content method may be, it is often a highly effective means of achieving educational development *as measured by current standards* (amount of knowledge acquired, degree and speed of proficiency in certain skills, etc.). It is effective in a static world if it is tested in situations in which the knowledge or codes or rules remain appropriate. Its effectiveness, however, is directly related to: (1) the degree to which the child responds to the rewards and punishments administered by the teacher, parent, or other outside source; (2) the degree to which the child has accepted the standards of the training agent (i.e., provided the child feels "it is good to learn anything if my teacher (or Mommy) wants me to"); and (3) the degree to which the matter being taught is relevant to the child. Very often, as we all know, one or more of these conditions are not met, with results that may range from the poignant or semicomic to the tragic. Let us give just one example of what happens when a student is not interested in a specific presentation of material. Note that the student described was interested in learning the traditional subject matter of educational curricula but in a way that is relevant for his own needs.

THE POOR SCHOLAR'S SOLILOQUY

No, I'm not very good in school. This is my second year in the seventh grade, and I'm bigger and taller than the other kids. They like me all right, though, even if I don't say much in the classroom, because outside I can tell them how to do a lot of things. They tag around me and that sort of makes up for what goes on in school.

I don't know why the teachers don't like me. They never have very much. Seems like they don't think you know anything unless they can name the book it comes out of. I've got a lot of books in my room at home, books like Popular Science, Mechanical Encyclopedia, and the Sears' and Ward's catalogues—but I don't very often just sit down and read them through like they make us do in school. I use my books when I want to find something out, like whenever Mom buys anything second hand, I look it up in Sears' and Ward's first and tell her if she's getting stung or not. I can use the index in a hurry.

In school, though, we've got to learn whatever is in the book and I just can't memorize the stuff. Last year I stayed after school every night for two weeks trying to learn the names of the Presidents. Of course I know some of them like Washington and Jefferson and Lincoln, but there must have been thirty altogether, and I never did get them straight.

I'm not too sorry though, because the kids who learned the Presidents had to turn right around and learn all the Vice Presidents. I am taking the seventh grade over, but our teacher this year isn't so interested in the names of the Presidents. She has us trying to learn the names of all the great American inventors.

I guess I just can't remember names in history. Anyway, this year I've been trying to learn about trucks because my uncle owns three and he says I can drive one when I'm sixteen. I already know the horse-power and number of forward and backward speeds of twenty-six American trucks, some of them Diesels, and I can spot each make a long way off. It's funny how that Diesel works. I started to tell my teacher about it last Wednesday in science class when the pump we were using to make a vacuum in a bell jar got her, but she said she didn't see what a Diesel engine had to do with our experiment on air pressure so I just kept still. The kids seemed interested though. I took four of them around to my uncle's garage after school and we saw the mechanic, Gus, tear a big truck Diesel down. Boy, does he know his stuff!!

I'm not very good in geography either. They call it economic geography this year. We've been studying the imports and exports of Chile all week, but I couldn't tell you what they are. Maybe the reason is I had to miss school yesterday because my uncle took me and his big trailer truck down state about 200 miles, and we brought almost 10 tons of stock to the Chicago market.

He had told me where we were going, and I had to figure out the highways to take and also the mileage. He didn't do anything but drive and turn where I told him to. Was that fun! I sat with a map in my lap and told him to turn south, or southeast, or some other direction. We made seven stops, and drove over 500 miles round trip. I'm figuring now what his oil cost, and also the wear and tear on the truck—he calls it depreciation—so we'll know how much we made.

I even write out all the bills and send letters to the farmers about what their pigs and beef cattle brought at the stockyards. I only made three mistakes in 17 letters last time, my aunt said, all commas. She's been through high school and reads them over. I wish I could write school themes that way. The last one I had to write was on, "What a Daffodil thinks of Spring," and I just couldn't get going.

I don't do very well in school in arithmetic either. Seems I just can't keep my mind on the problems. We had one the other day like this:

If a 57 foot telephone pole falls across a cement highway so that 17 3/6 feet extend from one side and 14 9/17 feet from the other how wide is the highway?

That seemed to me like an awfully silly way to get the width of a highway. I didn't even try to answer it because it didn't say whether the pole had fallen straight across or not.

Even in shop I don't get very good grades. All of us kids made a broom holder and a bookend this term and mine were sloppy. I just couldn't get interested. Mom doesn't use a broom anymore with her new vacuum cleaner, and all our books are in a bookcase with glass doors in the parlor. Anyway, I wanted to make an end gate for my uncle's trailer, but the shop teacher said that meant using metal and wood both, and I'd have to learn how to work with wood first. I didn't see why, but I kept still and made a tie rack at school and the tail gate after school at my uncle's garage. He said I saved him ten dollars.

Civics is hard for me, too. I've been staying after school trying to learn the "Articles of Confederation" for almost a week, because the teacher said we couldn't be good citizens unless we did. I really tried, because I want to be a good citizen. I did hate to stay after school, though, because a bunch of us boys from the south end of town have been cleaning up the old lot across from Taylor's Machine Shop to make a playground out of it for the little kids from the Methodist home. I made the jungle gym from old pipe, and the guys made me Grand Mogul to keep the playground going. We raised enough money collecting scrap this month to build a wire fence clear around the lot.

Dad says I can quit school when I am fifteen, and I am sort of anxious to because there are a lot of things I want to learn . . . and as my uncle says, I'm not getting any younger.[2]

The above illustration is only one of a host of observations as to what results when there is a breakdown in the conditions upon which content learning is dependent. There are others: from Henry Adams' comment (1918), "The chief wonder of education is that it does not ruin everybody concerned in it, teachers and taught," to James Agee's observation (1966) that there is "no attempt to counteract the paralytic quality inherent in authority," to Edgar Friedenberg's position (1967) that it punishes creativity and independence.

The past two decades, particularly, have not been easy ones for the American educator. Back in the late 1950s, a few people were asking why Johnny couldn't read as well as Ivan. Hardly had educators time to formulate an answer when the culturally disadvantaged child was suddenly thought about, stimulating people to inquire why Johnny could read better than José. Nor was there any respite in sight for the harassed educator; even as he grappled with the dilemma of the underpriviledged student, a new groundswell of criticism was building by individuals who questioned why Johnny or José should want to read what the schools offered at all. Perhaps the cruelest charge of all was that leveled by critics who saw the teacher and the school as the sole culprits for our educational woes when it is, in fact, the society as a whole that is responsible and that directs its professional educators to impart knowledge, skills, and polish in the traditional manner.

Our position is not that content learning is wrong, per se, nor that it should be junked wholesale and the "rascals turned out." We will argue, however, that the more or less exclusive use of this method creates very serious problems, particularly when educating children for the second half of this century. We believe that the current content-learning emphasis must be reduced. It is our contention that this particular educational method and philosophy is only a *part* of healthy development. There are certain outcomes or consequences—cognitive and personality—that can be quite damaging to the individual when confronted *exclusively* with content-oriented education.

THE CONSEQUENCES OF CONTENT-ORIENTED EDUCATION

What are these outcomes? The more or less exclusive use of content-learning procedures fails to provide the individual with the ability or means to deal with and solve new, unexpected problems; to handle novel, rapidly changing situations. In other words, one of the "by-products" of the traditional learning approach is a low level of adaptability or creativity in a changing environment because the child has had little opportunity to generate any new information himself. Thus, when the problem situation changes, he is poorly equipped conceptually; that is, he does not "think for himself."

Indeed, far from acquiring skill in generating new information, the student learns just the opposite. If he is to adapt well to a content-learning environment, he must always—as we have discussed earlier—look to an external source or authority for the ready-packaged knowledge and solutions to his questions and problems. At the same time, he learns to look externally for the judgment (standards) of his behavior; he begins to think of "good" and "bad" and "right" and "wrong" by what others say. And, in time, he learns to think of the world and his own behavior by reference to external sources: blaming others or outside forces for what goes wrong, praising these same forces when things go right.

A child taught exclusively by content-learning procedures and judged by content-learning criteria also learns to structure his world as more certain and less ambiguous because this mode of adapting helps ensure his gaining rewards from the training agents—the external source. After a period of time, the child begins to lose the intrinsic sense of wonder and interest, and the curiosity to learn, which were his when he came into the world. External forces have now become the usual motivation ("I should get good grades because that means I can get into college") to encourage acquisition of information. Perhaps it is this loss of intrinsic wonder and curiosity that explains Torrance's finding that children lose some of their creativity in the early school years (the so-called "fourth grade slump") (Torrance, 1968).

Let us make it clear, however, at this juncture that these content-inspired types of behavior and ways of responding are *not* the purpose nor the intent of the well-meaning teacher or parent nor, certainly, are they part of any school's educational objectives. "No teacher has ever said: 'Don't value uncertainty and tentativeness. Don't question questions. Above all, don't think!' The message is communicated quietly . . . and effectively through the structure of the classroom: through the role of the teacher, the role of the student, . . . the arrangements made for communication, the 'doings' that are praised or censured" (Postman & Weingartner, 1969).

One does not have to dig very deeply into most current educational settings to see what we mean. Take a walk through almost any school, even those most recently built with their carpeted halls, pleasantly colored walls, and elaborate equipment. The rooms are designed so that the children sit in rows facing the teacher. The arrangement hardly encourages them to learn about the ideas and conceptions of others; there is little opportunity for the child to search—he is already headed toward the teacher, the external authority source. Look under his desk. You will find books that give him all the information, answers, and ideas according to given "subject" (content) areas—geography, mathematics, biology, etc. Look around the walls. Above, below, and between the attractive mobiles and collages are lists to be committed to memory. Look at the blackboard. Written there by the teacher are questions designed to make the student "think": "Give two reasons why the dinosaurs became extinct, . . . Name three animals that estivate; three that hibernate . . . What is the main mountain range in North America? . . . Why was Utah first denied statehood in the Union?" In some schools, you can also find special machines to speed up the acquisition of this knowledge. Look in the teacher's desk. You will find instructional guides in each subject matter filled with such implicit assumptions (none of which has any actual verification and many of which have evidence to the contrary) as the "fact" that *content* is most effectively dispensed by a "course of study"; that there is a "logical sequence of strengthening a traditional pedagogical approach in these ways. imparted; that compartmentalizing instruction keeps the "content pure" (Harris, 1962). You will also find all sorts of tests; each designed to discover how much content (how many "right" answers) the child has mastered. Most of the rooms (including the library) are designed to hinder or restrict individual search. Indeed, more often the rooms echo with the teacher admonition, "Work quietly alone, and don't ask your neighbor for 'the answer'. If you want help, come to me." Unintended as such practices may be, they do remain as persistent by-products of this sort of educational orientation.[3]

One of the major consequences of content-oriented education is becoming increasingly apparent today. The current system of education is extrinsic, as we have discussed. As long as we continue to view educational development in this way, it is not surprising that school improvement is translated into adding to or bettering the extrinsic resources: more classrooms, more teachers (lower student-teacher ratio), more paraprofessionals, more audio-visual equipment, etc. Some of these solutions may have little evidence to support them (as the Coleman Report revealed), and some may enhance an extrinsic system and the amount of content learned, but as the taxpayer is only too aware, the cost can be burdensome if not excessive. Moreover, even if the dollar factor could be ignored, we still cannot escape the major consequence of strengthening a traditional pedagogical approach in these ways. The more we reinforce or improve the system, the more we enhance its negative consequences! That is to say, we run even greater risk of producing the extreme forms of those problems that emerge from a sole reliance on content learning:

1. Education that often does not prepare a child to be "free" that is, to cope effectively, resourcefully, and flexibly with the demands of his changing world.

2. Education that usually dampens the child's intrinsic interest in learning and coping and substitutes instead external motivation and control of his behavior with the result that:
     (a) There is often a high degree of boredom with the formal educational process.
     (b) There is a high degree of risk that problems and "subjects" selected for study, and the work materials chosen, will not be relevant to the students.

3. Education that fosters a tendency to avoid uncertainty and ambiguity and, concomitantly, to view the world as fixed.

4. Education that often leads to a dependency relationship between training agent and trainee: where the child or student comes to perceive the parent or teacher as "omnipotent."

5. Education that frequently fails to develop an internal sense of causation in the child ("I am master of my own destiny").

PERMISSIVENESS AND CONTENT LEARNING

The aforementioned deleterious consequences of content learning have not gone unrecognized. When the reliance upon external sources became severe enough, a substantial number of educators and parents reacted to the more extreme authoritarian methods being practiced in classrooms and playrooms. Although the popular interpretation was otherwise, it is important to note that the proponents of the "progressive education movement" did *not* eschew the bulk of the traditional educational philosophy. Their particular concern was the tendency to endow the training agent with a nimbus of omniscience and dominance that engendered an atmosphere of authoritarianism on the one hand (agent), and passivity/hostility on the other (child). It was agreed, and rightly so, that the more excessive forms of discipline and control associated with content learning were harmful to the child's cognitive and self-development, particularly the latter. Thus, the idea of the "permissive environment" was introduced into American education and childrearing. These early pioneers (Dewey, 1910; Hall, 1914; Kilpatrick, 1925; Rogers, 1951[4]) were sensitive to the price that is often paid by molding children to a set of predetermined templates: the reduction of spontaneity, interest, curiosity, and creativity at a time when our society was in real need of such attributes in its citizens.

Unfortunately, their efforts failed to produce the hoped-for revolution. Although many parents and teachers were persuaded by and often practiced permissiveness, such well-intentioned efforts bore a kind of fruit that was as bittersweet in its own fashion as that produced by the more authoritarian environment. The place of the omnipotent training agent was subverted by the omnipotent child. The process went full circle; children who had too much direction now had too little or none. How did such an exquisitely ironic state of affairs come to be? Primarily, because the educators and parents who embraced the philosophy and practice of "permissiveness" lacked two essential factors—a *method* and a *criterion*. The two are obviously closely related, but let us deal with each separately in order to emphasize an important point.

First, the permissive environment was never clearly defined. Child development was thought of as a natural, unfolding process that should be interfered with little or not at all. Generally speaking, there was a presumption that child development is predetermined; that is, the development of the individual parallels the evolution of the human race. This was translated into the idea of "readiness for learning"—a child cannot learn anything until he is "ready" maturationally for it. Thus, the role of the training agent is to provide a warm, accepting, reflective environment in which the child, left to his natural propensities, will grow and develop along optimal lines.

While this view (based to a large degree on a growth principle or self-actualizing tendency—Rogers, 1961; Maslow, 1962) contains a strong appreciation of natural evolvement and relevancy to the learner, it also fostered a kind of extreme permissiveness which prescribed that the parent or teacher should refrain from setting goals for the child or from channeling his behavior into directions that the "parent" or "school" desired. That is, it often encouraged a laissez-faire approach to child rearing and education—the less interference and manipulation, the better.

It should be pointed out that some highly skilled psychotherapists and counselor-teachers have succeeded in creating for some patients and students an environment in which the training agent sets only broad limits and remains nondirective while the learner is free to explore (Rogers, 1961). But most teachers have found it difficult, if not impossible, to accomplish the same with the great majority of American children (particularly when they have to teach large groups of them at a time).

For most parents and educators, permissiveness, *in practice,* became a world in which the child was all-powerful. By giving up all controls, the adult oftentimes seemed at the mercy of the whims and dictates of his charges. And the omnipotent child, lacking direction and guidance, created an environment of license rather than freedom.[5]

Even so, the permissive approach to content learning may have spared our society those outcomes resulting from an even higher degree of saturation of authoritarianism: aggressiveness, narrow-mindedness, intolerance, and conventionalism. Unfortunately, however, it produced yet other problems in youth: lack of commitment, lack of respect for the rights and views of others, lack of faith and trust in authority, and the growth of an unhealthy attitude toward freedom. A major weakness of the laissez-faire interpretation of the permissive environment is that, although it allows individual freedom of choice and action, it fails to provide situations in which the child learns to deal with conflicting standards. The all-powerful child experiences freedom but never learns responsibility. He learns to equate freedom with "doing your own thing," and that becomes the *only* thing to do; he learns to think of freedom as doing what is pleasurable, satisfying, and amusing to him without regard to the occasional necessity of postponing immediate gratification for long-term gains. This orientation, while possibly less harmful to society as compared to the extreme outcomes of the authoritarian forms of traditional training, nevertheless remains maladaptive in a world crying out for respect for others, individual responsibility, and the capacity to work with others.

The second problem encountered by those taking a less authoritarian approach to content learning was direction of purpose: the goals of permissiveness were never clearly specified as separate from those of traditional content learning, at least as far as measurement was concerned. While some may argue that such criteria as increased creativity, spontaneity, individual worth and interest were clearly stated as important to "progressive" childrearing and education, we point out that these criteria were *never* measured or used as an objective yardstick to plot the course of a child's development in the home or at school.

In fact, the heart of the problem was this: when training agents introduced the permissive environment, they continued to use the traditional educational criterion, the content criterion. This was rather unfortunate, because the practice of permissive techniques was far more suited to accomplishing process goals rather than content goals. Thus, at the age of six, little Johnny was still expected to know his three Rs—regardless of whether they had to be drilled into him or he had discovered them himself at a rate that satisfied his own curiosity. The result of such a state of affairs is sadly evident in the history of the permissive environment within traditional content-centered education. It is a history of vacillations from the more authoritarian content-centered environment to the child-centered permissive approach and back again. The object or goal of permissive education was not to increase the amount of content a child assimilated (clearly, such a method—if properly introduced—would be expected to reduce at least the amount of rote memorizing a child did); yet the assessment of permissive education—the evaluation of its worth—was based on the traditional criterion: the amount of information known. Consequently, it is hardly surprising that when the traditional standard was used to evaluate the permissive vs. more authoritarian method of instruction, it was the former that came out the loser. Such findings always encouraged opponents of the permissive methods to demand a return to common sense, discipline, and the omnipotent teacher or parent.

And thus we come to a major point in this book. The problems confronted by the "progressive" educators remind us that *innovations in childrearing and/or education must be accompanied by new criteria* for defining and assessing its proper role in human development. Once a criterion has been established and methods devised to measure it, then one can proceed to develop procedures (i.e., educational environments) that will increasingly accelerate a child's progress according to this measure.

"What finally controls an institution are the values it holds for itself—the means which are used to determine whether or not the values are being attained through the efforts of the institutions. . . . This means, in baldest terms, the measurements which are used, for it is measurement which supplies the concrete specification of the behaviors desired and also the means by which to judge their attainment. Schools are controlled, finally, by the measures they want to make, can make, and do, in fact, make. . . . Traditional measurements are deeply rooted in school practice, as are the narrow . . . concepts on which they are based. New measures and concepts, sufficiently strong to compete with the old, are required. Tests are needed which include the new dimensions. . . . Apart from the creation of such measures, it is highly improbable that any general progess can be made in reordering education so that it serves the needs of the nation in cultivating the creativity of its general population" (Mooney and Razik, 1967).

It is our belief that the shortcomings experienced with permissive training procedures in home and at school grew out of their ill-defined methods and unfitting (illsuited) criteria rather than their basic premises, which were sound. A child should be able to benefit from permissive training, to grow and develop, assuming that such training is properly executed and assessed according to means congruent with the basic purpose or philosophy of such training. We will now turn to a hopefully realistic and operational strategy for achieving healthy intellectual and emotional growth in the child by utilizing a responsive (process-oriented) training environment.

SUMMARY

The philosophy and practices underlying content-centered education are presented. The pedagogical environment for content learning consists of a parent or teacher acting as a storehouse of information, a repository of concepts, rules, solutions, or units of knowledge that he selectively transmits to the child. The child, in turn, is expected to learn what the training agent teaches so that he may use such material at a later time. Many times, content-learning procedures are characterized by:

1. A fixed teaching pattern.
2. Emphasis on passive learning.
3. Limited student-teacher interaction.
4. Emphasis on external controls and motivation.

The consequences of content-oriented education are discussed. Unlike some contemporary critics, we do not feel such content procedures are always outmoded nor should they be totally discarded. It is suggested that such methods can be quite valuable and effective in preparing the child for certain types of situations and/or when used in conjunction with the newer process goals that we recommend. We do emphasize, however, that when taken alone, content methods do not supply the child with the creative outlook he will need to cope successfully with today's highly complex and rapidly changing world.

In addition to inadequately preparing the child to successfully adapt to contemporary society, content-centered education has these additional drawbacks: (1) The child comes to depend on others for his view of the world. Self-reliance is sacrificed in favor of reliance on others, and the child has no reason and little opportunity to develop his own information-processing skills. (2) The child is motivated to learn by externally defined and administered rewards and punishments rather than by an intrinsic interest in knowledge (a genuine love of learning). (3) It is often irrelevant to the child's interests. (4) It encourages the child to avoid or ignore ambiguities in his environment and to resist uncertainty. (5) It often leads to a dependency relationship between training agent and child: where the child or student comes to perceive the teacher or parent as "omnipotent." Such a state of affairs is often conducive to the development of authoritarian educational methods that are easily implemented in such circumstances.

An attempt by "progressive" educators to eliminate some of the harmful consequences of content-centered education, specifically, authoritarian training methods, are reviewed. These reformers introduced the "permissive" environment into education and childrearing as a reaction to the more autocratic forms of content learning. They argued correctly that the extreme forms of discipline and control associated with much content learning arrested the child's cognitive (intellective) and personal development. Unfortunately, the efforts and good intentions of these antiauthoritarian reformers produced difficulties almost as severe as those they hoped to overcome. The omnipotent teacher was replaced by the omnipotent child who, once faced with too many directives, now had not enough.

It is argued that the shortcomings experienced with permissive-training procedures in the home and at school grew out of their ill-defined methods and incorrect criteria rather than their basic premises, which were sound. It is pointed out that a child should be able to benefit from permissive training once such training is properly executed and assessed according to procedures congruent with the basic philosophy of that training. The following chapters are devoted to an updated and operational strategy for achieving healthy intellectual and emotional growth in utilizing the responsive (process-oriented) training environment.

"Is the purpose to know a certain number of things, or is it to become capable of creating and inventing new things?" J. Piaget

3. Education as Process Learning

There are two facets of human development that are always present in any learning situation be it a group of toga-clad youths strolling beside their tutor or a pigtailed ten-year-old trying to put together the parts of a jigsaw puzzle. There is the cognitive or intellective facet on the one hand, and the self or personality facet on the other. In most educational environments, one component advances at the expense of the other. We have already discussed in some detail each of these aspects of educational development as they relate to the content-learning approach. Let us now look at process learning. For the purposes of clarity, we shall first consider the cognitive component, saving discussion of the personality (self) aspect for Chapter 5.

THE PROCESS ENVIRONMENT

Education as content learning puts great emphasis on the child's ability to select the appropriate "prepackaged" rule or concept that he has previously learned or committed to memory and to use this solution or concept accurately and efficiently. In what we call *process learning,* however, the child is *learning how to put things together. The accent is upon his learning to generate his own concepts. That is, he practices the kind of thinking (information processing) required to create concepts by combining information in response to the challenges and demands of a given learning situation.* Herein lies the core difference between the two philosophies. Process learning focuses on increasing the child's capacity to be self-sufficient in generating new questions, conceptions and outcomes as opposed to the utilization of ready-made answers. Concept formation and utilization are at the heart of process ability.

Process learning emphasizes expanding the range and increasing the effectiveness of an individual's concepts and ways of dealing with the world rather than with the storage and repeated duplication of behavior already well ingrained (Biggs, 1968). It focuses on behavior that is adaptive and flexible. In process learning, the child is judged by his *information-search behavior* (the amount and type of information he acquires through his own efforts and the pattern of his search) and *how well* or effectively *he uses that information to handle problems and deal with his environment. The role of the training agent (teacher or parent) in process education is to shape the environment so that the youngster must search for information and use it to form his own ideas, thus encouraging the child to develop those cognitive skills (process ability) he will need if he is to generate his own rules and form his own concepts.* By contrast, the role of the teacher or parent in content education is to anticipate what problems the child will encounter and to give him a set of rules or concepts that will "answer" those problems.

Process ability, like any other ability, can be thought of as extending along a scale from low to high. While our neurological potential sets limits to the level of conceptual functioning we are capable of reaching, process ability is a function of our training history. An individual rarely achieves the same level of functioning across all aspects of a given area. In the domain of athletics, for instance, he may achieve a high level of skill in such "individual" sports as skiing or golf, but a much lower level in body contact games such as football or lacrosse. The same is true of process ability. We can, as a result of our training, be high in one area (e.g., in conceptualizing about people), and low in another (e.g., conceptualizing about religion). We shall see that the same student can be low in process ability in social studies but high in process ability in mathematics. Even though we may reach a high level of proficiency on the knowledge or content criteria over a broad range of subjects in school or college, few of us reach a very high level of process ability across many subject areas.

In process-centered education, the training agent encourages the child to develop the cognitive skills he will need to generate his own information and set of rules in coping with his environment.

To this end, the child in a process learning environment is encouraged to:

1. Actively explore his world.

2. Seek out new and relevant information in problem solving.

3. Be capable of organizing units or attributes of information from several vantage points (combining and recombining the units so they can be differentially viewed).

4. Connect, organize, and utilize multiple concepts or perspectives in different ways in thinking and decision making.

5. Be flexible and willing to change behavior if a better way of behaving is discovered.

6. Remain open to new information even though it might be stressful.

7. Consider conflicting points of view in arriving at decisions.

8. Be sensitive (aware) to changes in his environment.

9. Be adaptive—be capable of changing behavior rapidly to match the contingencies of a rapidly changing environment.

10. Make complex value judgments. (While it is important to learn to generate alternate conceptions of a given set of information and to weigh these perspectives in different ways in order to consider all alternative answers, it is also necessary to make judgments, to close down and say, "Out of all these alternatives, I accept this organization of the information as correct at this time." Value judgments generated in this manner are more complex and adaptive in changing situations than are rigid, single-minded values.)

As can be seen, the child in process learning is expected to actively seek out information in his environment, to put it together in new and meaningful ways in problem solving, and if not successful in coping with a situation, to be able to modify his concepts and try again. Throughout such efforts, it is understood that the child is primarily responsible for charting and executing his own course of action: his concepts and decisions are self-made, not the products of external training agents.

The more the educational environment offers opportunities for the child to practice processing information—as opposed to acquiring the finished product of someone else's thinking as in content learning—the greater the likelihood he will develop his own procedures for dealing effectively with the world.

THE BEHAVIORAL CORRELATES
OF INFORMATION PROCESSING ABILITY

Let us take a moment to describe the personality characteristics of the person high in information processing ability. What kind of a person is he? What kind of behavior can we expect of him? Will he behave differently from individuals with lower levels of processing ability? If so, why?

Each person perceives the world and responds to it in his own unique way. Man is an information-processing organism—a filter screen standing between incoming stimuli and behavioral responses. What he sees, how he sees it, and his reactions to perceptions are all dependent on his "cognitive model" for viewing the world. Such a "mental regulatory program" is necessary because man is constantly bombarded by far more stimuli than he could ever consider, and he must have a way of choosing which components of his world he will attend to.

It is our belief that the person's level of information-processing skills determines just how complex (creative) his view of the world will be. In other words, an individual's level of information-processing maturity will affect *what* he perceives in his world and *how* he utilizes those perceptions in behavior. Like intelligence, the level of a person's information-processing skills is a joint outcome of inherited potential and environmental training.

How do people differ in their perceptions of the world? According to our theory (Schroder, Driver, and Streufert, 1967; Karlins, 1968), individuals with well developed information-processing skills have (as compared to persons possessing less mature information processing skills) a greater number of perceptual categories for receiving information about the world, and more combinatory rules or concepts for organizing such units of information. When we speak of a person possessing "a greater number of perceptual categories for receiving information about the world" we are referring to his ability to *generate more information* relevant to his needs. When we refer to "more combinatory rules for organizing such units of information" we are speaking of the individual's ability to *organize conceptually* and use materials in a creative manner in problem solving. These two hallmarks of well-developed information-processing skills—*information generation* and *concept formation* (and utilization)—will be the abilities we want to measure (provide criteria for) in our schools.

A person lacking mature information-processing skills has few degrees in freedom in his dealings with the environment—he uses simple and fixed rules in designing courses of action. He is not able to generate a diversity of information about a particular subject, and cannot effectively organize information in a variety of ways for decision-making purposes. Individuals with low levels of information-processing ability are often intolerant of ambiguity, dogmatic, rigid, and closed-minded. They are dependent on external authority and externally defined rules; and often are inflexible in their attitudes and categorical in their thinking.

A person with mature information-processing skills, on the other hand, can modulate his transactions with the environment. He is, in many ways, a mirror opposite of the person lacking skills in information processing: he has many degrees of freedom in dealing with the world; he is an active manipulator of his environment; he generates his own rules for coping with problems; and he is attuned, adaptive, and flexible in the face of change and uncertainty. Such an individual has greater or multiple ways to organize sensory inputs, to mediate them, and to respond to them; he is capable of entertaining and processing alternative explanations of an event, and seeks diversity and discrepant material in his information processing. With such skills, one might begin to appreciate how the mature information-processing organism would be better suited to successful survival in a rapidly changing, complex world; better prepared to cope with different groups he encounters; and better able to generate decisions more appropriate for a diverse and changing society.

One way of summarizing the difference between individuals high and low in information-processing skills is to imagine two persons, both with 140 IQs, one possessing a poorly developed information-processing ability, the other a well-developed information-processing ability. We would call the person with immature information-processing skills *intelligent* and the mature information processor *intelligent and creative.*

LEVELS OF INFORMATION PROCESSING

Let us turn from a general description to a specific example. Up until now we have been speaking broadly of differences between individuals "high" and "low" in process ability. Such a procedure is useful for descriptive purposes—for communicating to the reader the kind of behavioral differences that can occur between persons varying in process ability. However, from a theoretical and measurement standpoint, it is important to keep in mind that information-processing skill is not a dichotomous variable (either "high" or "low") but rather, a continuous one: with infinite gradations possible along a scale from extremely low to extremely high. The nature and range of this variation in information-processing ability will now be illustrated by an example. In this example we will be looking at six different teachers involved in planning and making a decision about the same student. All the teachers have had *equal,* ample opportunity to observe the following salient features of the student's behavior: (1) his grades are borderline failure; (2) he seems to spend his time reading and building models of motors; (3) he actively organizes his peers to join him in the pursuit of his interests. In the following example note how the teachers—equal in their knowledge of the student's behavior—differ in their ability to utilize effectively that knowledge in arriving at the best possible way to help the pupil with his school problems. Such differences in information utilization are at the heart of individual differences in process ability.

Teacher A. This individual has very little process ability. He would be at the low end of a scale denoting information processing skills. Teacher A engages in *categorical thinking* when making judgments about students. He categorizes students as "good" if they have A or B averages and "bad" if they have lower grades—whatever their value. That is, he lumps students into two groups on the basis of a single attribute—grades—and his judgments about the students are made solely on this basis. Faced with the problem of planning for our student who attained a grade of D, Teacher A would naturally focus on requirements for getting a higher grade—the sole basis for his thinking about academic planning. Given the single attribute of "grades" as the basis for thinking and judgment, the teacher would delineate the things "good" students know and can do and would require the "bad" student to emulate their behavior. His decision would most likely involve requiring our student to devote more time to doing the things the "good" (A and B) students do. The simple conceptual foundation of his thinking locks him into a way of evaluating students and then into particular kinds of solutions for overcoming their problems.

Teacher B. Teacher B is slightly higher on the information-processing continuum. When faced with the dilemma of what to do with our D student, he engages in *unidimensional thinking.* Like Teacher A, he also uses a single attribute—grades—to evaluate students but, unlike Teacher A, he is able to scale or rate students along the entire continuum extending from low grades to high grades. This teacher perceives *degrees* of "good" and "bad." He can make finer distinctions (discriminations) between students on the basis of academic performance. His judgments are less categorical than Teacher A's. In planning for the D student, Teacher B (like Teacher A) would still focus on the academic component in solving the problem and his decision would involve inducement for the student to work harder on the acquisition of knowledge directly associated with getting higher grades. Compared to Teacher A, Teacher B can extract slightly more information about students—even though both are using single-attribute thinking. For example, Teacher B is able to value a student for progress from a grade of D to a grade of C whereas, for Teacher A, the student would still fall into the category of "bad."

In grappling with the problem of the D student, Teachers A and B consider only his academic performance in their decision making. Other information about the pupil—his interest in mechanics and his peers—is ignored. The two levels of information processing represented by the two teachers are illustrated in Figure 1. In all single-attribute thinking—regardless of the nature of the dimension used—the criteria for judgment is simple and fixed. Judgments tend to be bipolar and are accompanied by a great deal of subjective certainty. There is little room for doubt or uncertainty and no motivation to stimulate further information search and/or information utilization. Such thinking ignores much relevant information and constricts the range of solutions to problems.

This kind of bipolar, bifurcated thinking is not restricted to examples or laboratory situations; it is, unfortunately, quite common in all parts of our society today. It is not restricted to the uneducated, the young, or the unsuccessful. A substantial body of research in personality and social psychology demonstrates that a good many of us think at this level when making judgments, for instance, about other individuals, groups, or nations. Persons prejudiced against blacks often lump all Negroes together at one end of an evaluative scale or dimension (good—bad; friendly—hostile). Other people will group a number of different countries into categories on the basis of a single, bifurcated scale of communist—noncommunist (or "democratic"). Although such thinking is economical, it is maladaptive, particularly in changing situations, because of the high probability that relevant information along other dimensions is being ignored.

Teacher C. At the next higher level of information-processing ability, il-

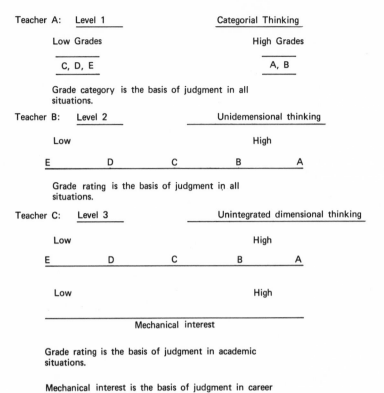

Teacher A: Level 1 _____   Categorial Thinking _____

Low Grades   High Grades

C, D, E   A, B

Grade category is the basis of judgment in all
situations.

Teacher B: Level 2 _____   Unidemensional thinking _____

Low   High

E   D   C   B   A

Grade rating is the basis of judgment in all
situations.

Teacher C: Level 3 _____   Unintegrated dimensional thinking _____

Low   High

E   D   C   B   A

Low   High

_____
               Mechanical interest

Grade rating is the basis of judgment in academic
situations.

Mechanical interest is the basis of judgment in career
situations.

Fig. 1   Single attribute thinking.

lustrated here by Teacher C, two dimensions of information about the student
are taken into account—but the two kinds of information are used in isolation. This type of information processing may be referred to as *unintegrated*
or *compartmentalized dimensional thinking.* Teacher C uses the dimension
of "grades" and the dimension of our student's interest in mechanics. In considering the student, Teacher C judges him low academically and high
mechanically—but the two are not brought together in making judgments or
planning (Figure 1).

This kind of thinking is common in everyday life. In general, information
about student interests is not taken into account in academic planning. One
dimension—grades—is used to evaluate and plan in the academic domain
and another dimension—interest—to evaluate and plan in the career domain.
In this way, and due to this kind of compartmentalized thinking, academic
programs often become divorced from career development. The presence of
unintegrated dimensional thinking is also observable along a time continuum;
for example, we use certain religious dimensions in our thinking on Sunday
and ignore these dimensions for the remainder of the week.

The person who can utilize unintegrated dimensions of information is capable of making judgments that are less absolutistic than those produced by individuals employing categorical or unidimensional thinking. For example, in the single-dimensional thinking exhibited by Teachers A and B the judgment "bad" (based on a student's grade of D) spreads to all aspects of his life. For Teacher A, our student is categorized as "bad" and is judged negatively in all situations—academic, career, and so on. Teacher B can make finer discriminations concerning academic performance, but he, too, is guilty of using grades as the metric for assessing the student's worth in all walks of life. Teacher C uses more than one kind (dimension) of information—and, even though they are unintegrated, this means that the student can be judged negatively in one situation (academic performance) and positively in another (skill in mechanics). Teacher C's "third level" of information-processing ability represents a move away from absolutism and all the cognitive and emotional characteristics associated with simplistic levels of thinking (Chapter 5).

Teacher D. At the fourth level of information-processing ability Teacher D *combines or integrates* two dimensions of information about the student (academic performance, mechanical ability) in order to gain a broader perspective about him in the academic setting. At this level of thinking (judgment), the teacher actively forms a concept about our student by *combining* different kinds of information. Teacher D keeps different kinds of information salient and utilizes them to form a hypothesis—a perspective or a concept about the student as a basis for planning and judgment in the academic domain. Here there is movement away from the simpler forms of thought. The gathering of different kinds of information about a person or an event is a part of the judgmental process. Furthermore, conceptual "work" is required to put the different kinds of information together into some meaningful idea.

Given the information about our student's low grades and high mechanical interest, Teacher D might arrive at the concept that he is "unchallenged" by the academic environment. At this level of information processing, note how the two kinds of information are held in focus and used to generate a concept that is being used as a basis for planning. This is illustrated in Figure 2. In using this concept as a basis for academic planning, Teacher D might well decide to have our student study his difficult subject—history—via the Industrial Revolution.

The formation of concepts permits us to bring more information to bear simultaneously in planning and judgment. From a philosophical standpoint, integrated multidimensional thinking represents a break with the "essence" or "entity" approach to human nature. Concepts are really hypotheses—they are tools (or vehicles) for making particular kinds of judgments; judgments that do not imply fixed characteristics of people or events.

Teacher E. Concepts vary in their "informational richness." Some concepts might be based on two types of information (Teacher D) and others on three or more different kinds of information (See Teacher E, Figure 2). In taking the social interest information into account—the information that our student

Teacher D: Level 4 _____   Uniconceptual thinking _____
                                                        (2 dimensions)

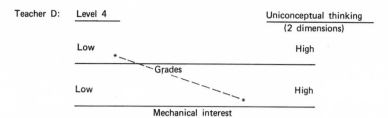

The concept of "unchallenged," made up of 2 scale
values (ratings of information (low grades, high mechanical
interest) is used as the basis of judgment in the academic setting.

Teacher E: Level 5 _____   Uniconceptual thinking _____
                                                        (3 dimensions)

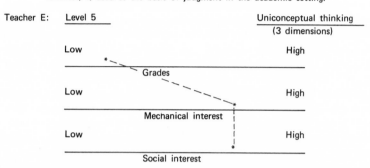

The concept of "unchallenged," made up of 3 scale
values of information (low grades, high mechanical interest
and social interest) is used as a basis of judgment in the academic
setting.

Teacher F: Level 6 _____   Multiconceptual thinking _____

Concept 1. ____ "Unchallenged by academic environment."

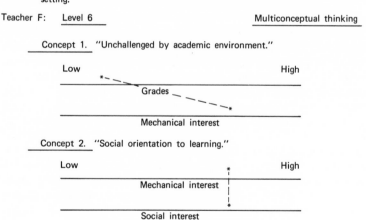

Concept 2. ____ "Social orientation to learning."

Two concepts formed on the basis of 3 scale values
of information (see above) are used as the basis of judgment
in the academic setting.

Fig. 2   Multidimensional thinking.

organizes and works closely with groups of his peers in pursuing his mechanical interests—Teacher E has combined more information into the concept of "unchallenged by the academic setting." This additional information will have an impact on the concept Teacher E creates and the decision he generates from it. For example, he might encourage the student to study the social and political implications of technological development over the last 200 years.

Multidimensional conceptual thinking permits us to bring more kinds of information to bear on our judgments. To be effective, it implies the presence of information search and concept formation in decision making. However, single-concept thinking has serious limits and must be understood as a stage or a step toward the higher goal of complex information processing (see Teacher F below). Single-concept thinking sets limits upon the amount of information that can be applied to making a judgment. There is a neurological limit to the number of units or attributes of information that can be combined into a concept. This number is surprisingly small—perhaps seven at the outside limit (Miller, 1956—but considering the conceptual "work" required to form concepts with many kinds of information, most everyday judgments are based on concepts combining less than three or four attributes.

The limited number of units one can combine into each concept causes a serious difficulty. In single concept thinking, there is the danger that a certain important piece of information might have to be ignored if many different kinds of information are relevant. (The information processor literally cannot "hold in" all the information at once.)

There is also a tendency for a single concept (hypothesis) to become fixed. This is the primary problem with this kind of thinking. In order for a concept to be adaptive, the information making it up would have to change regularly when conditions are changing—but this is unlikely to happen. Research indicates that once a concept is formed in a single-concept system, it tends to remain unchanged. The concept—once formed—becomes our hypothesis. As such it determines what we observe. In a single-concept system we tend to become identified with our hypothesis—we become ego involved and pay attention to those classes of information that support our beliefs and that maintain concepts.

The great majority of our social and human problems are based on our compulsive tendency to engage in uniconceptual thinking—to cling to the use of outmoded concepts. In the interpersonal domain, our thinking about ourselves, our peers, or our teenagers is often based on concepts formed years ago. Much of our current thinking and judgments in the field of foreign affairs and education is also. The challenge of education is to move information-processing ability beyond this level.

Teacher F. The highest level of information-processing ability will be referred to as *multiconceptual thinking*. This level is illustrated in Figure 2 by Teacher F. In this example, Teacher F holds the three kinds of information about our student in focus and forms true concepts from this information. One hypothesis (concept) is based on two kinds of information—low grades and high interest in mechanics and the other on the basis of interest in mechanics and high interest in working with his peers in pursuing this interest. In the first concept, the dimensions of grades and mechanical interest are weighted highest; in the second concept (social orientation to learning) the dimensions of mechanical interest and social interest weighted highest.

In planning for our student, Teacher F will take both concepts into account. He will design a program in which the student can feel challenged (e.g., study the impact of the Industrial Revolution on social and political life), *and* create an academic environment in which he can work most efficiently (e.g., form teams to develop reports and produce models).

In information-processing terms, there is a critical difference between thinking that rests on a single rule (concept) and thinking based on multiple rules. In the multiple-concept case, the person can take different selections of the information into account. Let us examine briefly the advantages and disadvantages of such multiple-concept thinking.

First, multiple-concept thinking is uneconomical when the appropriate kinds of information and the weights necessary to produce the best solution are already known. Under these conditions, a single rule can be written or learned that tells which information to use. On the other hand, multiple-concept thinking is advantageous when the amount of relevant information in an environment is too high to be subsumed and remembered under a single, given rule. Given complex environmental conditions, it becomes adaptive to form multiple concepts that select different or overlapping kinds of information. In this way, we form different kinds of overall impressions, perhaps from different standpoints. In the example, Teacher F used two concepts ("unchallenged by academic environment," "social orientation to learning") in dealing with the D student. Such a strategy permitted her to use more information in judgment. In a number of studies, we have shown that individuals with higher information-processing ability (i.e., persons who characteristically use multiple-concept processes) used more relevant information as the information load increased in a complex tactical task (Streufert and Schroder, 1965).

Multiple-concept thinking is most advantageous in situations that are changing and in which the problems are complex. The development of new concepts opens up new hypotheses about a situation, raises new questions. This process acts against the development of rigidities—the use of outmoded concepts in changing situations.

Forming new concepts can also create uncertainty and conflicting judgments. By generating conflict or discrepancy, the person is in a sense able to *motivate* himself and to create *interest* in exploring these conflicting possibilities. This is called *intrinsic motivation* and may be contrasted with extrinsic motivation—motivation or interest maintained by the promise of an external reward. Intrinsic motivation reaches its highest level in multiple-concept thinking but can be operative at lower levels as well (this is discussed more fully later in the chapter).

We would like at this point to reemphasize our belief that the development of information-processing ability from the more common single conceptual level to the multiconceptual level should be the major goal of education. As we move toward this goal, man will edge closer to gaining the complex processing skills he needs to achieve a meaningful life in our tumultuous times.

MEASURES OF INFORMATION-PROCESSING ABILITY IN EDUCATIONAL SETTING

It is the *ability to generate categories,* scales, or dimensions *for coding the flow of information and to use selected organizations of* these different kinds of *information in a flexible manner* in decision making that *is the psychological foundation of a person's adaptability to change. It is this information-processing capacity—so neglected in content-centered education today—which we propose be the primary focus of education in the future.*

But how does one go about measuring process variables such as information generation and conceptual organization? We propose that information-processing ability be assessed with a set of measures that are different from those currently used to determine content-learning proficiency in our schools. Let us look at some possible measures that could be used in a process educational environment.

As we have already indicated, at the higher levels of information-processing ability, a person is able to extract more kinds of information from a given environment—from a movie, a debate, a trip, or a story. Higher-process ability implies that the person can engage or evoke multiple concepts that direct search to a broader range of dimensions of information. Therefore, one way to assess information-processing ability is to place a person in a situation that presents a stream or sequence of events; for example, a movie of geographic and climatic conditions. To ask him: (a) to list observations that he believes relevant to identifying the area (flora, fauna, rainfall, topography, etc.); (b) at intervals, to require him to make hypotheses (concepts), as many alternatives as he can, about the location of the area he is observing. Here, the contrast with content criteria is quite clear: instead of asking the child to recall geographic facts about regions, he is given a stream of geographic information and asked to select relevant information, to take various selections of this information in order to form hypotheses, and—where possible—to assess the value of a chosen course of action.

The "process grade" the student would receive would be based on the breadth and relevance of categories observed, and the relevance and range of hypotheses generated. In order to assess another important component of information-processing ability, the test film could move from one region to another so that the information is changing. Here we would assess the speed at which the new information is observed and the rate of change in the nature of the hypotheses. Such a test is most discriminating when its speed (rate of information flow) is optimal. At low rates, fewer demands are placed on information-processing structures and, at higher rates, the enivronment is beyond the limits of conceptual capacity. All tests of information processing should be checked for information load as a step in their development.

In a related method, information-processing ability is measured via the questions a child generates. This test is essentially an information search task in which the child seeks to solve a problem by asking questions. In solving problems, it is now recognized that asking the relevant questions is the difficult task—once a question is formulated, finding its answer is relatively simple. The child or adult is able to ask new questions if he can formulate a new way of conceptualizing a given problem.

An anecdote will illustrate the point. One of Albert Einstein's friends visited the famous mathematician regularly. Week after week he would be ushered into a study where Einstein sat amidst a mass of papers. One day Einstein's friend asked him if he was getting closer to a new answer, and Einstein replied, "No, I'm still unable to ask a new question." Creative problem solving begins with the formulation of new questions that point the way to new observations and, eventually, answers.

In many ways, the concept of information generation through asking questions is related to "productivity" notions of creativity. One popular approach to measuring creativity via psychological testing is to define creativity operationally as proficiency in generating responses to a word or words, such as "Uses for things" (Guilford, 1965; Wallach and Kogan, 1965). In this framework, the degree of creativity is a function of the number of responses or products produced. The higher the productivity the higher the creativity score on the examination.

This productivity notion of creativity can be related to the generation of questions in a process-centered problem situation. Keeping in the Guilford "generation of alternatives" conception, one might contend that the more questions an individual is able to ask about a given problem, the higher the likelihood of his solving it. In other words, the more active an individual is in his information search of a given problem domain, the greater his chances will be of finding the problem's best possible solution. Recent evidence indicates there is a relationship between Guilford's measures of "divergent" thinking and question-asking behavior in problem-solving environments. In a 1967 investigation, Karlins, Lee, and Schroder found that students who were able to produce a number of "uses for things" on Guilford's test of creativity were also the individuals who displayed the most active and diversified information search in three problem-solving tasks (they asked the most questions and searched in the most categories).

Information-generation tests, designed to measure a person's information-search skills, could be constructed for process-study units used in the school curriculum. These examinations would consist of well-prepared problems the student might reasonably expect to confront in the subject area. In social studies, for example, the student might be asked to write down all the questions he would want to ask in order to solve a problem such as the best place to locate a new school or airport.

The questions generated by the student would be scored in terms of the number of different kinds of information sought. By different kinds of information, we mean classes of information that are grouped under different concepts. For example, in a problem concerning placement of an airport, the student might ask ten questions all concerned with geographical dimensions. Another student asking an equal number of questions, might, however, ask about geographical considerations and other factors such as population density and public opinion. The first student has based his inquiries on fewer dimensions than the second student.

It would be the challenging and important task of the test constructor to determine (through pretesting) the kinds of information that students ask, and the concepts or perspectives they utilized to arrive at their inquiries. Once this was accomplished, a child's breadth and depth of information search (the number of perspectives he utilized, and the frequency of inquiries asked within these perspectives) could be determined. The depth measure would indicate the importance of any given perspective to the student (by observing how many times a particular perspective was used to generate questions).

To illustrate what we mean when we are talking about tests for measuring information generation and information search, let us refer to the Community Development Exercise, a complex, problem-solving task that utilizes the Inductive Teaching Program (Karlins, 1967. See Chapter 4 for a discussion of the Inductive Teaching Program as a pedagogical environment). In the Community Development Exercise, students were required—through asking factual questions—to find the best possible way to build a hospital, with the cooperation of local natives, on the South Seas island of "Wabowa." In this particular task, there were 57 categories of information available concerning various aspects of the "Wabowan" culture (see Appendix A). In his information request, where the student must ask questions in order to gain information he feels is relevant for solving his task, it is predicted that the information-processing maturity of the individual problem solver will influence the ways in which he searches for information. Behaviorally, these differences will be manifested in two ways: (a) the number of information domains the student employs in dealing with the complex task that confronts him (number of the 57 categories sampled) and (b) the frequencies with which each information domain is used in information request (number of times each of the 57 categories is sampled). The first way refers to the *breadth of information search* (across categories); the second, to the *evenness, or breadth and depth of information search* (relative frequency of sampling within and between categories). Breadth of information search is measured by determining the number of the 57 categories sampled (with analysis controlling for possible bias due to differences in questioning frequency); evenness of information search is measured through utilization of the $\hat{H}$ (uncertainty) statistic (Senders, 1958).

It is quite easy to confuse the difference between breadth and evenness of information search. Possibly we can dispel the confusion by pointing out it is possible for individuals to sample the same number of categories (identical breadth of information search) asking the same number of questions and still have different *patterns* of information search (evenness of category sampling). This is illustrated in Figure 3. In this example, two students, F and S, exhibited the same *breadth* of information search (they both asked 100 questions in 20 different categories), but their *evenness* of information search was quite different: student F has asked almost 50% of his questions in 10% of the categories he utilized, while student S has distributed his questions more evenly across the informational domains he sampled. In terms of uncertainty analysis one can say that Individual S, in comparison to Individual F: (1) displayed more evenness of information search across and within the 57 categories; (2) generated more uncertainty, in the statistical sense (the number of binary questions that must be asked in order to ascertain his behavior).

We have just tried to show how a student's pattern of information search—one important component of process ability—can be tracked and measured. Such measurements can be utilized, of course, for a variety of problem-solving tasks. Other indicators of information-processing ability could also be assessed. For example, the student could be asked to generate concepts (hypotheses) about the hospital task and to arrive at an overall decision. The greater the number and range of relevant hypotheses and the extent to which these are used in arriving at a decision, the higher the process grade he would receive. The concern here is with the way an individual *utilizes* the information he has gathered to arrive at an answer to his problem. In the Community Development Exercise, for example, the student is asked to write a "position paper"—utilizing the information he has gathered to suggest a solution to his problem; his idea of "the most effective way to get the hospital built on Wabowa with the cooperation of the natives."

The score or "process grade" on the information-generation test can also provide important feedback for the student. The teacher can present the pupil with a profile portraying his pattern of information search—showing him what types of questions he failed to ask and the perspectives which he ignored. In this way, the test scores can be used to portray graphically to the student the deficiencies and strengths in his information generation—providing him with relevant training in information processing.

Another procedure for giving the student "feedback" on the strengths and deficiencies in his information search is to let him ask questions about a problem, arrive at a solution based on the answers to his questions, and then have him discuss his solution with a group of his classmates who have arrived at their own decisions through the same procedure. In discussing their different conclusions (and with groups of four or five students there is bound to be different solutions to the same problem) each student comes to see the soundness and shortcomings of his own information processing. (For other extremely important benefits to be gained by such group interaction, see p. 63).

In an information-search process "test," the number of perspective-relevant categories a student explores is a measure of the number of per-

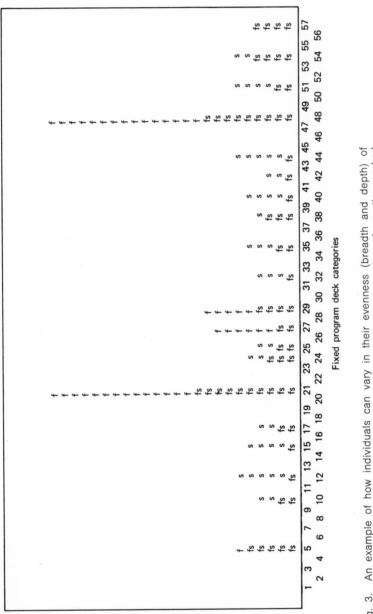

Fixed program deck categories

Frequency of category sampling

Fig. 3. An example of how individuals can vary in their evenness (breadth and depth) of information search when their breadth of categories sampled and number of questions asked are the same. In this case individual "f" has asked almost 50 percent of his questions in 10 percent of the categories he utilized, while individual "s" has distributed his questions more evenly across the informational domains he used.

spectives he can "take on" and use as a basis for inquiry. It should be pointed out, however, that a wide range of ready-made perspectives taught by the content-centered method will also produce a high score on the breadth-of-information-search measure. To avoid this problem, the test developer can do two things: (1) make sure that the test situation is novel—so that ready-made perspectives supplied by others will not be of great aid to the student (the test must still be relevant to the general academic topic, however); (2) present a changing problem situation. For example, one could give a description of a community along with a problem to be solved, and have the student generate questions. Then a change could be introduced in the problem that would open up a new set of perspectives and have the student generate additional inquiries. Such a format will provide an opportunity to measure change in the range of perspectives adopted by the student as the situation changes.

To illustrate: in a social-studies unit, the student could be presented with a description of a primitive, mythical island culture (whether or not he knows it is mythical is immaterial; the important point is that it must not be identical with a culture he has previously studied). The information in the description would be factual (i.e., no conclusions would be drawn for the student) and would cover areas such as physical environment (e.g., plant and animal life, topography, and rainfall); customs (e.g., religious rites and family organization); economy (e.g., principal products and property division), and so forth. All the information would indicate that this culture is highly dependent upon heavy rainfall to support the cultivation of coconuts and, as a result, much of the life of the society has been built around this principal product even though there are other resources available on the island. A conflict problem is also presented, namely, that through climactic change, the rainfall has decreased and will no longer support the cultivation of coconuts and a totally agrarian way of life. It is the student's task to "tell a story" as to what island life would be like under the new conditions.

The student is encouraged to ask as many questions as he wants, but he is not allowed to ask questions: (1) on material that is already covered in the information given to him and (2) that will give him a ready-made answer. That is, he may ask a question such as "What is the birth rate on the island?" but he will not receive an answer to a question such as "What will the people use for money if they no longer have coconuts to barter?" This is done so that the answers will represent scale values of information that can be tracked and measured. The student must use these scale values, as many as possible, to arrive at hypotheses and "solutions" on his own (Phares, Gardiner, and Schroder, 1971).

Tests of this type (they can be varied, of course, as to complexity and difficulty depending upon age and grade level of the students) serve a dual function: they assess an individual's level of information-processing ability, and then can be used to teach individuals how to process information more effectively (and, by the way, teach him a lot of "content" at the same time). It is this dual role that makes them particularly useful in the classroom.

It is becoming increasingly recognized that the investigation of a student's question-asking behavior in problem solving is a good way to assess his information-processing skills. This is indicated in the following quote of Rimoldi and his associates at the Loyola Psychometric Laboratory: ". . . during the last seven years a new approach to the study of problem solving has been developed. Originally it was applied to the study of the medical diagnostic process and more recently it has been tried in a variey of fields with promising results. The basic assumption underlying this approach is that complex mental processes can be described and evaluated by the sequence of questions asked by a subject in solving a problem. The main interest lies in the study of the process, rather than in the exclusive interpretation of the final answers" (Rimoldi et al., 1963).

Information-search tests can measure an individual's information-processing ability in a given area, but they are not easy to construct. They are not the kind of thing teachers can be expected to put together during lunch hour. Some tests of process ability in certain subject areas will have to be devised by specialized groups (corporations or research institutes in educational administrations), since the major task of the test developer is to provide a pool of information concerning the chosen problem or situation that is extensive enough to provide suitable answers to the majority of questions that might be asked by a student in his information search. Thus, while it is the student's task to explore a given environment through questions so that he can acquire a sufficient body of facts to form hypotheses, it is the responsibility of the test constructor to provide the student with the means of making such conclusions possible.

In creating this necessary body of information, the test developer can employ one of two (or both) procedures: (1) he can anticipate the types of questions that might be asked and prepare his materials accordingly; (2) he can pretest his instrument, letting a large group of students generate as many questions as they can about the problem, and then prepare a set of answers based on these questions.

As we have indicated earlier, the best test would utilize a changing environment, so that ability to change concepts and the dimensions of search (as the situation changes) can be assessed. This is a central skill in information-processing ability.

Information processing is a very complex ability. Initially, the measurement of this ability will be difficult; but with increasing experience and research, measures should become increasingly refined and accurate.

INFORMATION PROCESSING AND ABILITY TRAINING

Information-processing ability, as we have defined it, is a measure of the maturity of thinking. In more mature thinking, a person can use more and more information; he is good at developing strategies for organizing information in flexible ways so that particular concepts (rules) do not become fixed and unchangeable. It is our contention that despite certain genetic limits, this ability is modifiable and can be developed—*even in adults*—given appropriate environments. Our aim at this point is to show that modification is possible— the educational environments for process learning will be discussed in Chapter 4.

The issue of trainability is important because recently some have expressed the opinion that differences in reasoning ability may be genetic and unmodifiable by the general educational process. Specifically, Jensen (1969) has argued that reasoning ability is generally lower for the black population and that this is not simply a result of difference in social class and training because the result holds for the children of middle and upper class Negro children whose reasoning ability scores as measured by IQ tests are lower than lower class white children.

Since a number of effective criticisms of this view are available (e.g., Hunt, 1969), we will not attempt a comprehensive critique here. However, as Hunt argues, it is often difficult to distinguish between the effects of genetics and early experience. He has shown that a stimulus-poor nursery environment can produce a permanent decrement in mental functioning. When the environment was enriched, the level of functioning increased.

Information-processing ability grows as the child practices coding—as he learns to construct categories or scales or dimensions along which information (e.g., about objects or people) can be received. The ability increases as he explores stimulus-rich environments (optimally complex environments). Stimulus-poor or overly complex (overly stimulating) environments depress development.

In two carefully controlled concept-training experiments (Lee, 1968; Carrington, 1970), it was shown that higher levels of information processing could be induced, at least temporarily, by short-term training. In both studies, individuals were trained to use either two or three kinds (dimensions) of information to scale or code information about applicants for a job. Each group was then split again; half were trained to use a single concept (rule) that instructed the person to take all the information into account (either two or three different kinds), and half were trained to take two different selections of the information into account (i.e., to use two concepts). That is, four different groups of individuals were given four kinds of training. One group was trained to use two kinds of information and to weigh these two scale values in one way (one conception). A second group was trained to think of the applicants using two kinds of information and two weighting schemes (two conceptions). A third was trained to use three kinds of information (dimensional scale values) and one conception, and a fourth group to use three kinds of information and two conceptions.

Following training, information-processing ability was measured in two ways: (a) subjects were asked to write an essay comparing and contrasting the four applicants in terms of their overall suitability for the job. Higher information-processing ability was measured as a function of: the richness of the concepts; less frequent tendency to use bipolar descriptions; the number of relevant conceptions used to compare and contrast applicants; and the degree to which alternative conceptions were taken into account in judgement. (b) Subjects who disagreed on overall rankings by a constant amount were seated at a table and asked to come up with a unanimous judgement. Higher information-processing ability was indicated by greater openness to understand the conceptions of the other person, more probing to discover the conceptions of the other people, and a greater consideration of multiple conceptions in arriving at an overall judgement.

The results show that direct training influenced measures of information processing in two ways:

A. As the number of dimensions of information increased from two to three (regardless of the number of different concepts used), the resulting information-processing ability increased.

B. As the number of different concepts used increased from one to two (regardless of the number of dimensions of information), the information-processing scores increased.

Before the training, individuals were tested for initial general level of information-processing ability in thinking about people. Even though direct training increased information-processing scores for all persons, individual differences in initial level still persisted. However, these differences were less than they were at the pretraining level.

THREE IMPLICATIONS OF PROCESS LEARNING

It is our belief that several benefits will accrue from exposing children to a process-centered education—benefits that will be expressed in a more creative, psychologically healthy child:

1. The Development of Intrinsic Motivation in Children. Motivation refers to the factors that initiate and direct behavior—that energize and guide the individual's actions. What is it that stimulates a child to seek out information? To solve problems? To learn? In short, what makes a child *want* to learn? Contemporary education is not greatly concerned with such questions—as long as the child *does* learn. The development in the child of a healthy self-directed and self-sustaining interest in learning and experiencing is a neglected goal in most present-day schools. Evaluation of the student is almost exclusively focused on such considerations as how well he writes, how many historical facts he knows, how neat he is, how he fits into the teacher's routine, and not on how *interested* he is in trying to write, learn history, and so forth. The teacher views the child as striving to attain standards that he or she holds, and insists the child is "good" if he pursues these goals.

Many middle-class children learn to seek high standards of academic excellence for their own sake. They are rewarded by their parents and teachers for adopting and achieving these standards. But not all middle-class children and very few children from the ghetto and lower socioeconomic classes learn to achieve rewards in this way. One only need walk into a classroom in any American school today to see that most students do not have an intrinsic, self-sustaining love of learning. Take away the teacher's power to reward and punish and there would be very little learning indeed! Why is this? Why are so many students uninterested in their classes? Children are not born uninterested. On the contrary, children are excited to learn to talk, walk and play; to experiment, explore and invent. They are certainly capable of intense interest. Why, then, the loss of excitement, of love for learning? "The contemporary history of our culture leads to a general observation that parents [and, we would add, "schools"] spend the first ten years trying to restrict this exploration, this eagerness, this curiosity—the second decade of their experience with the child trying to rekindle the spark which they have so successfully extinguished" (Anderson, 1965).

According to our point of view (which is shared by Hebb, Hunt, Biggs, and others) there are two types or systems of motivation:

A. *Extrinsic motivation.* When a child is motivated to perform a given act by outside reinforcement—when his behavior is initiated and directed by the administration of rewards and punishments by an external agent (parent or teacher)—we speak of his activity as being extrinsically motivated. By this we mean that the child performs a specific way due to forces outside of himself. In content-centered education, extrinsic motivation is extensively supplied—the child is given information to assimilate and is rewarded for using this information in appropriate ways.

B. *Intrinsic motivation.* Here a child acts independently of extrinsic rewards —he does not have to depend on the reinforcements supplied by others—he has his own "built in" system of rewards and punishments. His motivation is based on his ability to sense discrepancies or mismatches in the various perspectives he considers. These discrepancies—these incongruities in the environment—act as stimulators. By generating discrepancy or conflict, the person is able, in a sense, to *motivate* himself and to create *interest* in exploring these conflicting possibilities. Such discrepancies (provided they are at an optimal level—neither too great nor too small) not only are the instigators or energizers of the motivation but also help to sustain it. Nor is such motivation associated solely with the accomplishment of a given task; it also operates in more general areas ("behavior dominated . . . by the thought process that is not *fully* organized—one that is achieving new organization. . . ." Hebb, 1949, p. 229). Such a preference for the more complex (increasing incongruity or discrepancy) may well explain "competence motivation" (White, 1959, 1960) or the "urge to mastery" (Hendrick, 1943). It has been demonstrated, for instance, that 10–12-year-old children, when given block-design problems, tend to spend more time with the more complex problems and that children will repeat "games" with surprising outcomes more often than "games" with expected outcomes (Charlesworth, 1964).

To the child, information processing itself—the ability to see the same information in different ways—is motivating, stimulating, and worthy of effort.

"Meaning making" becomes a joy to him. Hunt (1970) refers to this as "motivation inherent in information processing." The child's ability to see conflicting discrepancies in his world keeps the "processing" in action. Note that effective process learning leads to the utilization of conflicting organizations of information as the major strategy in decision making.

When a person is highly skilled in processing information—when he has been trained in a process-centered environment that teaches him to see and appreciate discrepancies in his world—then he has the raw materials for generating his own motivation to inquire and learn. A person trained in information-processing can generate multiple perspectives that provide the means of experiencing discrepancies; such discrepancies provide the motivation to learn and generate more perspectives, in a never ending cycle.

When the individual is not skilled in information processing—when he has not been trained to generate multiple perspectives from the same information —then he requires extrinsic rewards and punishments to keep him stimulated. In content-centered education, where the child does not develop this potential to generate new perspectives and, instead, "gets along" with a simple information processing system, it is little wonder that extrinsic rewards are so firmly entrenched in the school system.

According to our analysis, the development of information-processing skills in the schools is necessary if we are to break out of the extrinsic system we are now in. No matter what changes we make in our educational system, the changes will fail if they do not facilitate the development of intrinsic motivation in the child. As Berlyne (1965) has noted, ". . . immense wells of intrinsic motivation lie within the normal child, which are capable of lending powerful support to the teacher's efforts when properly tapped but are all too often stopped up by traditional techniques of instruction."

2. The Development of Greater Potential to Adapt to Change. A person who is taught to develop his information processing skills—who learns how to generate multiple and relevant perspectives when confronted with a problem—becomes more adaptable (creative) in a rapidly changing environment. This is because he is taught to be an active manipulator and innovator in his world; to utilize information in new and meaningful ways in confronting his surroundings. The individual possessing mature information-processing skills is distinguished by his:

A. *Active and diverse information search.* The basic building blocks of any discovery are the units of information that a person can bring to bear in solving a given problem and, presumably, the more relevant information a person has at his disposal, the better are his chances of confronting the world in a creative manner. A person with well-developed information-processing skills is more likely to acquire "relevant information" because he has been trained to: (1) be *an active seeker of information* (rather than a passive receiver of information), and (2) *consider a greater breadth of information in solving a problem.* A person with multiple perspectives looks into "nooks and crannies" for information; he seeks a greater range and diversity of information in the environment. Thus, if material exists somewhere that can help solve a problem, the individual with mature information-processing ability is likely to uncover it.

B. *Creative utilization of information* (*concept-formation ability*). It is not enough to seek information actively and have it available. Oftentimes, to reach a creative solution to a problem, that information must be processed—put together—in new and meaningful ways. Consider a jigsaw puzzle: to have available all the pieces necessary to complete the puzzle is a prerequisite to solving the problem, but not a guarantee the problem will be overcome—first, the pieces must be *put together* in a manner that will provide a solution to the puzzle. So it is with problems in the real world: once information relevant to a situation has been amassed it, too, must be organized in a manner suitable to allow coping with that situation. The creative utilization of information refers to the process of information *integration:* the ability to generate combinations of informational units and interrelate these in a number of ways in problem solving. A person with developed information-processing skills (in comparison to individuals with less developed skills) brings more information to bear in problem solving because he has multiple concepts that allow him to utilize a broader range of information: organizing and unifying separate pieces of information into a new product.

C. *The critical ability to assess the value of a chosen course of action.* Once a product has been produced or a problem solved, an individual is left with the necessity of determining the effectiveness of that product or solution in relation to the situation for which it was intended. When one speaks of "the critical ability to assess the value of a chosen course of action" he is referring to the skill involved in deciding to retain, modify, or discard a given product based on its success in accomplishing anticipated (and unanticipated) tasks. The person with well developed information-processing skills is better able to judge the effectiveness of his decisions because he is capable of considering more information and more conceptions based on this information in assessing the adequacy of his judgments (see his actions in light of more contingencies) and is more likely to discover changes and problems.

Under conditions of rapid change—when new solutions are needed for new problems and old solutions are inapplicable for old problems—the person who willingly seeks new information, utilizes it in creative ways to solve problems, and accurately assesses the worth of those solutions is better prepared to make successful transactions in his environment.

The ability to generate multiple perspectives ensures the potential to modify the rules for combining information as situations change. Most of our problems of adaptation occur because we apply outmoded conceptual rules (e.g., attitudes that are no longer viable) to situations that require new perspectives. A person who has not developed his information-processing potential is often victimized by these outmoded conceptual rules because he lacks the ability to generate newer, more relevant rules for himself. He is often unaware that situations are changing and require new approaches; and even when he does become aware of environmental change, he cannot effectively generate new and perhaps more relevant perspectives and decisions in coping with such changes.

3. The Development of Self-Determined Value Judgments. When the goal of education in the home, school, or church is content learning, the child is taught other peoples' rules for dealing with the world. Sometimes these rules are given as if exceptions were never possible (e.g., "All men are evil," or "All American cars are poorly made"). Under more favorable conditions multiple perspectives are supplied (e.g., the child is taught two sides to an issue in history). In most cases, the statement of the value judgment (rule) is accompanied by the training agent's overall evaluation of it (which the child better learn!) and the final position the child should adopt with regard to it (which the child better accept!).

When such ready-made values are dispensed in education, they are either rejected (when the content-centered method is inappropriately applied) or assimilated to some degree by the child. Maintenance of these values rests on external control, and the child lacks the information-processing skills in that value area to modify it as a consequence of personal relevant life experiences. Further, the child is often incapable of conceptualizing shades of difference in a particular value (either a person has the value or he doesn't) and is unable to consider the impact of different value conceptions in making social decisions.

In process learning, values emerge and change via a continual process whereby alternative conceptions or perspectives are compared and tested, combined and evaluated. The preferred organization of perspectives emerges as the value. When the child arrives at a value through his own information processing, such values are more flexible (open to modification if new information in the environment warrants such change) than those "handed down" by external sources. An important part of process education is to teach the child that there is a point when he must stop generating alternatives just as there is a point when he must start such a process. Yet, this must be carefully done, because the child cannot be discouraged from considering alternatives—process education encourages the child to arrive at values by his own considerations. When a child arrives at his own values, he does so by evaluating the various outcomes of the perspectives he considers.

SUMMARY

Process learning is distinguished from content learning. In traditional content-centered education, the child develops the ability to select the appropriate "ready-made" codes or perspectives he has learned and use them accurately and efficiently when needed. In process-centered education, the child learns to generate his own codes, concepts, or perspectives—he practices the conceptual processes required to create his own ideas and answers to environmental demands. Process learning is devoted to increasing the range and effectiveness of a person's perspectives for dealing with the world—increasing his capacity to be self-sufficient in solving his problems (rather than relying on the dictates of others)—and not merely with the storage and replication of already well learned behavior. To this end, the child in a process learning environment is encouraged to actively seek out information in his environment, put it together in new and meaningful ways in problem solving, and, if not successful in coping with a situation, be able to modify his concepts and try again. The more the educational or home environment offers opportunities for the child to practice information processing—as opposed to acquiring the finished product of someone else's thinking as in content learning—the greater the likelihood he will develop his own procedures for dealing effectively with the world.

The behavioral correlates of information-processing ability are presented and discussed. It is argued that individuals with well-developed information-processing skills have a greater capacity to generate more information relevant to their needs and to conceptually organize and use this information creatively in decision making. To illustrate this point a hypothetical example is presented describing how six teachers varying in process ability might be expected to come to grips with a problem student.

A major portion of the chapter is devoted to describing measures of information-processing ability for use in educational settings. After briefly describing several process tests—their rationale, construction, relationship to "divergent" conceptions of creativity and scoring—a specific example of one such measure is presented in detail.

The chapter concludes with a discussion of three benefits accruing from exposing children to a process-centered education—benefits that will be expressed in a more creative, psychologically healthy child:

1. *The development of intrinsic motivation in children:* It is argued that content learning creates an extrinsic system of motivation in children. This is evident in the classroom: those children who are motivated to respond to middle-class oriented rewards and punishments (grades) will learn what they are told; those not motivated by such reinforcements (e.g., ghetto children) often become the casualties (dropouts of the system). We contend that information processing can be *intrinsically* motivating—that the very act of considering various informational discrepancies can provide its own rewards (and thus its own perpetuation). According to our analysis, the development of better information-processing skills in the schools is necessary if we are to break out of the extrinsic system we are now in.

2. *The development of greater potential to adapt to change:* A person who is taught to develop his information-processing potential acquires several skills necessary to adapt to change, including an active and diverse pattern of information search, the creative utilization of information and the critical ability to assess the value of a chosen course of action.

3. *The development of self-determined value judgments:* In process learning, values emerge and change via the child's own perspectives (which are constantly compared, tested, and evaluated) whereas they are often "passed down" to the child as dictates of the training agent in a content oriented environment. When the child arrives at a value through his own information processing, such values are more flexible (open to modification if new information in the environment warrants such change).

"Children need reassurance that it is all right ... to treat a task as a problem where you <u>invent</u> an answer rather than <u>finding</u> one out there in a book or on the blackboard."

Jerome Bruner

4. Educational Environments for Process Learning

If increased process ability is to become a goal of our educational system, radical changes will be required in our school environments. At the outset, most of these changes need not involve major capital expenditures for new equipment or additional teachers. This has already been tried. The basic requirement is something more difficult to attain—a change in attitude. Contrary to the common sense notions of many citizens and to the pleas of many teachers and administrators at both schools and universities, we do not need to impart more knowledge, we do not need to upgrade the disciplines. The priority at this stage is to build an environment in which the student takes an increasing share of the responsibility for learning; an environment in which he can develop higher level skills in integrating information while seeking the solutions to meaningful, interesting problems.

A GLIMPSE AT OUR CONTEMPORARY EDUCATIONAL ENVIRONMENT

One does not need to look very hard into most current educational settings to appreciate the pervasive atmosphere of content-oriented learning. Even in the newer buildings classrooms are self-contained, hermetically sealed boxes each separated from the other usually by age groups (first-grade rooms for six-year-olds; third-grade rooms for eight-year-olds, etc.). Study halls are noisy and used when there are no teachers to teach; libraries (if they even exist at all at the elementary school level) are too often small and restricted, and there are few, or no places for children to work together in small groups on a common task or to work alone in private.

In most schools, at almost any grade level, educational environments resemble the one portrayed above. It is only at the rudimentary levels of education—nursery schools and kindergartens—that changes in the traditional educational environment are noted with any frequency. It is rather ironical, but by our standards, the most elementary classes possess the most advanced educational procedures! That is, one must go to a nursery school or kindergarten before he can find process-learning procedures employed with any degree of regularity. Perhaps this turn away from content-centered education at these preprimary-school levels is necessitated because the school system has not yet had sufficient time to bring the child's behavior under extrinsic control (i.e., because extrinsic controls and rewards do not yet work too well with three- and four-year-old children). Yet, give these youngsters about two years and most of them readily learn to adapt their behavior to the extrinsic system of rewards and punishments of American education. Those unfortunate students who do not make this adjustment— who cannot respond to the traditional system of academic reinforcements— are considered "problems" and become dropouts from the extrinsic educational system.

In the traditional content-centered education, there is little room for a student who wants to explore on his own; to learn what he wants to learn when he wants to learn it. Little wonder! After all, a teacher with a fixed lesson plan and 35 students to lecture cannot very well afford to tolerate 35 different student-initiated courses of educational enrichment. Any student with his own ideas is quickly made to "see the light"—to want to learn what the teacher is required to teach. If the student is not willing to "see the light," then he is encouraged to look a bit harder by various forms of rewards and punishments. Sometimes these extrinsic directives are enough to discourage the child from pursuing his "deviant" behavior. If so, he might "adjust" to the education directed at him—even become a model student. But the price of such conformity can be extremely high: the loss of individual creativity or, even worse, the loss of individual identity. (This is well documented in the studies of Torrance (1968) where the price of classroom conformity is a reduction of individual creativity.)

Below is a poem submitted by a student who was forced to "fit into" the educational program of his school. The desperate eloquence of this student describes the pitfalls of content-centered education better than we ever could:

AND IF WE DO NOT CHANGE?

He always wanted to explain things
But no one cared
So he drew
Sometimes he would draw and it wasn't anything
He wanted to carve it in stone and write it in the sky
He would lie out in the grass and look up in the sky
And it would be only him and the sky and the things inside him that needed
    saying
It was then that he drew the picture
And it was a beautiful picture
He kept it under his pillow and would let no one see it
And he would look at it every night and think about it
And when it was dark and his eyes were closed he would still see it
And it was all of him
And he loved it
When he started school he brought it with him
Not to show anyone but just to have with him as a friend
It was funny about school
He sat in a square brown desk
Like all other square brown desks
And he thought it should be red
And his room was a square brown room
Like all other square brown rooms
And it was tight and close and stiff
He hated to hold the pencil and chalk
With his arm stiff and his feet flat on the floor
STIFF
With the teacher watching and watching
His teacher came up to him and spoke to him
She told him to wear a tie like all the other boys
He said he didn't like them
And she said it didn't matter
After that they drew
And he drew all yellow and it was the way he felt about the morning
And it was beautiful
The teacher came and smiled at him
"What's this?" she said. "Why don't you draw something like Ken's drawing,
    isn't it beautiful?"
After that his mother bought him a tie
And he always drew airplanes and rocketships like everyone else
And he threw the old picture away
And when he lay alone looking at the sky
It was big and blue and all of everything
But he wasn't anymore

He was square inside
And brown
And his hands were stiff
Like everyone else
And the things inside him that needed saying didn't need it anymore
It had stopped pushing
It was crushed
STIFF
Like everything else.

This poem was handed in by a student to his teacher. Although it is not known if he actually wrote the poem, it is known that this twelfth-grade pupil committed suicide three weeks later.

The question of what to do with an intrinsically motivated, self-directed student in an extrinsically motivating, other-directed educational program is not easily answered. We have seen that "winning" or attempting to win the pupil over to the traditional educational system might be a hollow victory indeed, achieved at the possible cost of individual creativity and personal health. Is there possibly another way out of the dilemma? Yes. Instead of making the child fit the school, let us begin to make the school fit the child. Let us turn classrooms into "workrooms with new criteria for noise, mobility, concentration, productivity (Biber, 1967)." By providing the student with a more open and diversified school environment—perhaps he will find the latitude of freedom he needs to express himself adequately. And, of course, it is our hope that as more and more students are exposed to such a flexible educational program they, too, will develop and wish to express their ability to be free and self-directive in their own educational progress.

THE IMPACT OF EDUCATIONAL ENVIRONMENTS

The problem with content training—the traditional educational environment— is not its effectiveness. As we have seen, if amount of knowledge acquired is the criterion, it can be, and is, very effective. *The problem lies in its side effects.* The real problem for psychology, for education, and for society is whether or not our almost total embracing of the content-learning philosophy is adequate as a vehicle for the positive intellectual and personality development of our children. The real question is: why are we so locked into the notion that educational development is the degree to which a child is able to conform to the objectives of others?

If the goal of education is the preparation of children to live a constructive life in a free society, the answer is that we must rid ourselves of such a notion. The question poses a serious choice—if we continue with an exclusive dependence on content-learning environments, we are really building a society in which an elite (such as educators and planners) dictate what children are to know and think. Let us not deny this. It would be a simple step to keep their behavior under control after they leave school, after being indoctrinated for sixteen or more years, plus the use of mass media and refresher courses if the elite should decide to modify the master plan. If our goal is to move society in this direction, then we should further embrace the content-centered, agent-oriented educational objectives. But if we do not wish to groom an elite who plan and control; if we intend to leave the style and direction of our future to an enlightened, creative citizenry—who are free and equal—then we must also provide environments in which children can grow in order to assume their responsibilities.

We must seriously consider the trade-off between giving the child freedom to exercise choice and responsibility and giving authorities the power to control the child's behavior. This is our dilemma today. We have met the problems of increasing educational demands by increasing content-oriented education via the streamlining of environments for that purpose. The effects are truly obvious in any school today, particularly in high schools, where we see the full impact of such environments.

Some children have become acculturated; they have become what the system was designed to build—a child who looks externally for what he is to know and think, who learns quickly in order to conform to the system of extrinsic rewards. They are the elite in this environment, and in a total content-learning system, they would become the planners for the next generation. But they have given up their freedom in our sense of the word; they have freedom in a culture where freedom is defined as one's ability to perceive and attain cultural rewards, but they are not free in a culture that places the responsibility for freedom on the individual. Conversely, those who do not conform to the controls are not at present being trained to exercise responsibility or to engage in mature thinking about social problems. As a result, the school oftentimes becomes a training ground for simplistic, revolutionary thinking.

It is not rare to find that children in the typical school have learned to live in two environments or two worlds. They have differentiated the school environment from their home environment perhaps because their home offers a more intrinsic environment. They conform to the school environment only to achieve its products—as a means, not as an end. They feel much is irrelevant to them; they are not interested in or committed to the formal classes. However, they do engage in creative work outside the school. For example, we have observed the interest and creativity shown by many youths who spend time in the university library where open stacks are available. They like to go there and follow up all kinds of subjects and projects not taught at school. They feel that this is the most important and meaningful part of their educational development. (This kind of behavior is not uncommon even in our colleges and universities where students are often heard to exclaim: "My most important educational experiences took place outside the classrooms.") Perhaps these particular kinds of students are fast learners in the content-learning sense, leaving time for individual work. But for many children, for a number of reasons, years of content learning have literally "turned them off." They either struggle through in various degrees of agony or drop out.

Children differ in the degree to which their personality fits the traditional, content-centered school environment. Many members of the aspiring middle class, particularly academically oriented parents, anticipate the nature of the school environment and begin to prepare their children to adjust to it at a very early age. The more a family builds or encourages a positive acceptance of such a system, the higher the probability the child will fit into it. But, in addition, the more consistently content-oriented the environment (control via rewards and/or punishments for conforming to external goals) the greater the chances that children who were not trained in the home to "fit into" such a system will fail to adjust to its demands. This problem is well illustrated in the plight of the lower-class child who has been often raised with interests, needs, background and goals that differ from the current educational "plan," that is, from the behavior required by the middle-class-oriented planner and teachers.

THE NEED FOR PROCESS ENVIRONMENTS

Is there a way to overcome the problems we have just outlined? We propose that an increasing part of the curriculum be changed from a content to a process environment. Such an environment would contain the following properties:

1. It would offer choice to the individual child. To an increasing extent, he will choose what he wants to learn, the speed at which he will proceed, and the way he wants to learn.

2. It would offer the child the opportunity to work alone—to search, inquire, hypothesize, try out, and to create a product on his own.

3. It would offer the child the opportunity to work with his classmates as a member of a team in solving significant societal problems; to recognize, accept and respect differences among individuals, and to develop via mutual understanding.

4. It would offer special process educational materials developed to give the child practice in information search, information utilization (forming concepts, testing hypotheses), and the use of feedback for modifying the ways he codes the environment.

The school environment will become more intrinsic and more process-oriented as one or any combination of the above are introduced. Maximum effects will be attained when all the properties exist. However, observations and evidence indicate that changes of considerable magnitude in intrinsic interest, intrinsic control of behavior, and information-processing ability can be expected with the introduction of process environments even on a modest scale.

Some readers may argue that most schools currently use intrinsic environments for some part of the curriculum. Certainly there are examples (e.g., Cole, 1971; Lippitt, Fox, and Schaible, 1969); there have been some special projects, some special classes and schools, and a great deal of experimental work—but in our experience and that of others (e.g., Silberman and Goodlad), the intrinsic environment is almost totally absent in almost all schools. If choice of what is learned exists, it is meaningless and relegated to unimportant matters; individual search, study, and choice is inevitably difficult in schools built for mass indoctrination: libraries are guarded, study halls are, in the main, noisy interludes between classes; serious group interaction for the development and solution of problems is rare, and development of process ability is rarely undertaken or assessed independently of content.

The introduction of intrinsic environments is not a simple matter. It will require a major reorganization of the whole school, even the relations between school and community. It requires a difficult role for the teacher. Although the individual child will choose his own problems, it is the teacher who must "set the scene" by choosing the process materials and situations; by guiding rather than telling the student what to do, or what "the answer" is; by posing contradictory information if the student is too quickly satisfied with his solutions. It requires a shift in attitude on the part of the teacher: she must accustom herself to the necessary uncertainty and ambiguity involved in process learning's search and choice; she must be able to accept, without anxiety, the individual variations in learning rate that are not based solely on mastery of content. It requires a new form of educational administration (Schroder, 1970). In short, lip service is not enough; radical reform is required. Organizational change is perhaps the initial step most schools would take. This problem will be discussed in the last chapter.

At this stage, let us focus on the changes we are trying to introduce. Each of the properties of intrinsic environments, and the role of content, will now be described in turn.

SIMULTANEOUS EXISTENCE OF CONTENT AND PROCESS ENVIRONMENTS

Throughout the book we have emphasized that we are *not* arguing for the total abolition of content-learning procedures. Actually they can be quite valuable, *when used in conjunction with process techniques,* in preparing the student for future eventualities. Most educators and parents would agree that a certain amount of knowledge (content) is basic. The definition of what and how much is basic will differ, of course, from school to school, over time (e.g., after Sputnik, there was a move toward emphasizing knowledge of mathematics and the physical sciences) and in terms of individual goals. For example, history becomes basic (i.e., in terms of the need for a broad content knowledge) for a person who is going to become a history teacher. This basic knowledge can be taught in either a process or a content environment.

However, in the process environment, it will be slower because the teacher cannot simply tell the child the sequences, hypotheses, and conclusions arrived at by historians. This is a point made by Ausubel (1965, 1966) in his assaults against "discovery learning" and the ability to solve problems. Ausubel states that such methods are "incomparably more time consuming than the method of verbal presentation," although he does concede that the so-called "discovery learning" techniques may be superior to verbal instruction (what he calls "reception learning") in terms of transfer of learning, retention of the material learned, and general understanding. We would add, in agreement with Gagné (1966), that it also promotes what Gagné calls a "love of learning in the learner" (intrinsic motivation). To continue with our example, the child must search for information and arrive at his own conclusions much as a historian does; then he can compare his conclusions with the conclusions of historians. This may be a good way to learn history, but it highlights the trade off if we are to adopt some process environments: there is a gain in process learning but a possible loss in the amount of content learning and the rapidity with which the knowledge is ingested. And we are proposing that the trade is required to bring back a healthier balance between content ability and process ability.

We do not believe that all learning should take place solely by "discovery methods" (where a learner discovers the solution without specific verbal help). We agree with Ausubel that there has often been a misunderstanding and certainly many an abuse of verbal instruction (reception learning); for example, an arbitrary presentation of facts to students without any explanatory principles, and the use of testing methods that require the pupil only to reproduce the ideas in the same context as they were presented. We agree that such abuses do not lead to "meaningful reception learning" and should be discarded. We also concur that "discovery learning" is not invariably meaningful but "depends on the conditions under which learning occurs" (see page 70, for example, and the discussion of some so-called process environments as they often are practiced). There most certainly is a place for meaningful reception learning in the repertoire of teaching approaches; so is there a place for meaningful process methods. Even so fierce a critic as Ausubel agrees that for children under twelve years of age (below the junior high-school level), it is preferable "to encourage pupils independently to complete the final step of drawing inferences from the data since the time-consuming empirical aspect of the learning must take place anyway"—and, further, that for any age, problem-solving techniques "have their place" in subject areas where: (1) the content matter is difficult to grasp on a verbal level as well as (2) in testing for the meaningfulness of verbal-reception learning.

The content environment should be maintained in our schools, to be used in conjunction with process learning. Our technological ingenuity can be relied upon to improve the methods of content learning—by using computers and automation to increase individuation, to help diagnose problems, and to streamline the learning process. Better methods should continue to be developed to teach such skills as reading, arithmetic, and languages.

As the facilities for process education are developed, some units will be taught using a combination of process and content environments (e.g., the use of computerized instruction following a period of discovering in a unit on history). Other units may be taught completely in an intrinsic process environment. The main point here is that, as Gagné put its, "learning by problem solving leads to new capabilities for further thinking. . . . Problem solving results in the acquisition of new ideas that multiply the applicability of principles previously learned" (Gagné, 1965). (Problem solving is used here in its broadest sense—not solely inductive reasoning as practiced by a scientist, but also the kind of thinking the *average* man uses many times during the course of a day; for example, a driver mapping his way through traffic rather than being pushed along by it.)

THE OPPORTUNITY FOR CHOICE

Basic to the development of intrinsic interest in learning is the opportunity to choose. To be effective, the child must not choose on the basis of control by the teacher, but through his own considerations. Of course, choice is always within limits; it can refer to the selection of a subject area (e.g., of a content environment for the study of American history) or a topic to study within an area (e.g., individual and group study of ethnic prejudice), or the way he wishes to proceed (e.g., individually, in a team, via a project, etc.).

Given the opportunity for choice, the child learns to see himself as the causal agent in his own development. In a constructive choice environment, the child learns to modulate his choice to the availability of resources; his choices become realistic and relevant with practice. They open up constructive ways for the student to influence the educational resources of the school. Student participation will remain fairly meaningless in an exclusively content-oriented environment. Participation requires individual responsibility, and it can only become meaningful in a "free" intrinsic environment.

Many will argue that offering the student such choice is unrealistic. On the one hand, they argue, it would fail because children would choose to do nothing or to do something irrelevant; and, on the other hand, even if the choices were feasible, chaos would result if 20 students in a class all selected different subjects and topics. In considering the first point, we agree that the exercise of mature choice requires interest and responsibility. In process terms, however, these are the goals. They are an outcome of process learning; they *are* an educable ability. If children in school cannot handle choice, it means that the system is failing. For the inexperienced older child, it will take time and patience. But it is our observation that even for these children, the selection of "nothing" (or of something unfeasible, which amounts to the same thing) will *not* persist.[6] That is, if he selects "nothing" or something he cannot do, he could be permitted to exercise that choice. Such children may be left in a room and encouraged to continue to search for a positive choice, alone or in groups. As boredom sets in, they will begin to do something; they will begin to make an intrinsic decision to do something. Any decision is a beginning of a mature process—whatever our views of the topic selected. For a particularly graphic description of the beginnings of the kind of environment we are talking about, the reader is referred to pp. 12–21 in *Freedom to Learn* (C. R. Rogers) in which the "experiment" of one sixth grade teacher is described.

Development is plotted not only by our evaluation of the academic excellence of the choice, but also by movement in the direction of making choices and in the vigorous pursuit of self-selected goals.

Initially, it will be hard for us to take this attitude to the student because we are so accustomed to an agent-oriented, externally controlled environment. Pilot developmental programs should be established to explore ways and means to allow for choice in the school system and the kind of organizational change and support required to "bring it off." As maturity in choice increases, the burden of education is moved significantly toward the child.

The second argument against choice, mentioned above, is that it will be unmanageable; it will lead to chaos because it is impossible to have hundreds of students all doing different things, or children of different ages wanting to do the same things. At first glance, this seems to be a serious organizational problem indeed. But, in fact, the problem instead will not be too much diversity of choice, but rather, too much conformity. Gradually, students can be presented with materials that may lead them in the pursuit of different problems. Or they can work in small groups on similar topics (see group processes discussed below). Inevitably, however, offering choice to the student will demand organizational, and later, architectural change.

A number of factors can be developed to support the experience of choice in educational environments. In the beginning, students might spend three two-hour periods per week on courses and topics of their own choice. If the choice is to be meaningful, the school will need to provide a bank of information, in addition to the library, which students can use. This information will refer to current events, statistics, survey data, speeches, policies, and other sources that are *relevant to various topics that the students select.* Such information banks could be built and organized by a community group and supported by students. Senior students could get credit for preparing information requested by more junior students at all levels. With the rapid development of on-line computer technology it is not unreasonable (from either a cost or supply perspective) that the "data banks" of information vital to the process-education orientation might soon reach each student via his own computer terminal.

THE OPPORTUNITY FOR INDIVIDUAL STUDY

The development of information-processing skills is partly an individual matter. Privacy is an important element in any educational environment, particularly in a process-learning situation, and it is often overlooked in our blind acceptance of mass learning methods. We must begin to design space in our school buildings for private work and information retrieval.

For individual work sessions (ideally combined with opportunity for choice), students need small cubicles that are fairly soundproof to which they can bring books and other materials for study in pursuing goals of their own choice. These cubicles could be similar in design to carrels found in many university libraries. Eventually, each work area would be tied into a closed circuit TV system and /or computer relay that would permit the child to request information that then would be transmitted directly to him. Such a system is costly, of course, but is an important means for providing the privacy and information that are so vital if the student is to develop individual responsibility for pursuing learning on his own and away from the all-pervading influence of the training agent.

THE OPPORTUNITY FOR SMALL GROUP INTERACTION

Effective process education requires time for the student to work alone. It also requires time for him to work in interaction with others. One of the real puzzles a visitor from Mars would experience (if he had read our books on growth and development and then studied the educational environments we design for our children) would be an almost total absence of the use of student-student interaction in the learning process. Having read Mead, Piaget, and the symbolic interaction literature and having observed children at play, he would be at a loss to understand why such a potent factor in learning and development was absent. He would seldom find small groups of students in our classrooms exchanging ideas and discussing differences.

The small-group environment (three to six children), where students bring their individually developed ideas and solutions regarding a common problem, is fertile soil for the development of information-processing ability. Here, in equal status, open discussion groups, students see how others select different information in approaching a problem (e.g., where to build an airport in the local area), how they form different conceptions and decisions. If the group is to arrive at a common, overall recommendation, then each member will learn to see the problem from the other members' points of view, and will receive training in forming decisions that are a superordinate product; that is, which are the outcome of many perspectives. Apart from its importance in developing information-processing skills—which is considerable—group interaction provides the individual with training in citizenship. It is in such group encounters that he comes to appreciate and respect differences of opinion and the rights of others.

Our visitor from Mars would be puzzled by the lack of group-interaction environments until he learned that such encounters, so important for learning, fail to bring masses of children's behavior under explicit control so that all produce a standard response. That is, they do not comfortably fit into a content-learning, extrinsic philosophy.

EXAMPLES OF ENVIRONMENTS FOR PROCESS LEARNING

We have spoken extensively about environments for process learning. In the next few pages we will present three such environments—two as new as the behavioral sciences in the 1960s; one as old as man himself.

1. Make Believe Play. Play, particularly "make believe" play, is an excellent example of an activity that is both intrinsically motivating and an important form of process learning. Make believe play provides a model for a process-learning environment; indeed, it is through such natural play activities that most American children learn what process skills they possess in social-cultural matters.

Why is play a form of process learning? Consider the child playing "house" or "school." He is taking on the role of another, for example, a mother or a teacher. He is developing a conception of himself and/or other aspects of the world from the mother's or teacher's perspective and vice versa. This in turn can lead him to ask new questions about himself and develop new conceptions of his appropriate role in specified situations. When playing with others, the child has the advantage of perceiving how the "other" reacts to his role and vice versa. He can compare what he knows about himself with what others think of him—put these pieces of information together—and try out a new "self" on those around him. In play, the child can act upon his environment (much as an inquiring scientist might) and see the results. He can ask his own questions and find the answers through play. As Erikson (1950) puts it, ". . . the child's play is the infantile form of the human ability to deal with experience by creating model situations and to master reality by experiment and planning."

The child at play is certainly engaging in process learning. His behavior is not "under the control" of a planner. He was not taught how to do it; he was not asked or forced to do it; yet he does it for hours, days, years. Through play, the child expresses his intense interest in defining his world and understanding his place within it.

Freedom to engage in play, especially make-believe, dramatic play, might well aid the child in developing the skills that process learning provides in the realm of social behavior, creative social adjustment, the ability to view the world from another person's perspective (point of view), and the capacity to make mature decisions regarding social actions and responsibilities.

Educators and psychologists are just beginning to realize the importance of play for a child's mental well-being and later development. Biber, Mitchell, and others at the Bank Street School have not only recognized the importance of dramatic play as "a special kind of tool for learning . . . which fuses the . . . conceptualizing of the groping child mind with . . . the forming inner self," but have also developed this recognition into a major teaching technique.

Neill (1960), in his milestone work at Summerhill, pleads with the adult to let children play. We could not agree with him more emphatically. Let us put it this way: the eventual capacity to be free critically involves the learning that takes place in interaction and play situations.

2. The Talking Typewriter. Alan Anderson and Omar K. Moore (1960) have designed an ingenious method for teaching children communication skills by process-oriented educational procedures. They have taken children who failed to learn reading and writing by content-centered methods and taught them such skills by use of a "talking typewriter." They have also used their typewriter with children who have never before been exposed to any academic instruction in reading and writing (usually prenursery or nursery-school age).

Here is how their system works. A child is escorted by one of his classmates into a small room containing a modified electric typewriter. The child is then left alone in the room—free to do or say what he pleases. There is no adult authority present and no extrinsic reinforcements controlling the child's behavior and "suggesting" what he should do. He can do what he wants to when he wants to. Eventually, the child's curiosity gets the better of him, and he approaches the typewriter. Soon he begins to play with it. What the child doesn't realize is that the machine in front of him is no ordinary typewriter. It contains several design features which have turned it into a self-contained process-learning environment! These features make it possible for the student to improve his English by his own information-search efforts.

For example, the typewriter can be programmed to teach the child the letters of the alphabet. This is done by providing the child with a visual image of each letter he depresses on the keyboard, accompanied by a voice pronouncing the letter out loud. Imagine the child's surprise when, upon pressing the letter "c," he hears a loud clear voice say "c," and sees the image "c" appear on a nearby screen. It is not long before the child is punching the keyboard at a rapid rate—fascinated by the resultant auditory and visual feedback he receives. The time span between the keyboard depression of a letter and its verbal description can be varied so the child can pronounce the symbol *before* the voice does. Under such conditions, children rapidly learn all the letters and numbers on the typewriter—calling them out loud and clear as they punch the keyboard, and then smiling as the mechanical voice confirms their predictions.

Once a child has a solid mastery of the alphabet, the typewriter is programmed to teach him words and (eventually) even sentences. This is accomplished by programming the keyboard so that letters can be depressed in specific sequences only: sequences that spell out specific words. Presume, for instance, that the word "CAT" was to be taught to the child. Under this condition the child would soon discover that he was unable to depress any button on the keyboard as he had done previously. In fact, the only buttons that would depress were labeled "C," "A," and "T"— and only when pressed in that order. At first the child is startled by this change in the rules of the game. He cannot understand why some of the buttons he presses are "locked" in place. But, with continued efforts, he soon (by chance) is able to successfully complete the "CAT" sequence; at which point he is in for another surprise. Once the "T" letter has been struck the child is presented not only with the visual and auditory feedback relevant to that alphabetic symbol but also the pronunciation "CAT." In such a manner the child learns to spell, recognize, and pronounce the words and sentences that comprise our language.

After taking his English "lesson" on the talking typewriter the child is returned to the traditional classroom situation and asked by the teacher to pronounce words projected on a screen. A critical finding here is that the child, when presented with a word he has never seen before, will use phonetics to try and "say" it. This indicates that the talking typewriter lessons allowed the child to generate the very complex linguistic rules of spelling. Such is the strength of a child's capacity to conceptualize—to process information—given the appropriate learning environment.

It is important to recognize that Moore and Anderson's "talking typewriter" method is not just another variation, however technologically sophisticated, of programmed learning. Other teaching machines utilize a rigid, detailed series of specific steps designed to lead the child to the predetermined "right answer." Such programs allow no variation, no possibility for search or exploration. The talking typewriter method, however, does preserve the essential possibility that the learner may come up with answers that haven't been thought of before. By so doing—by predetermining only the general environment—Moore and Anderson's system retains the essential variables of individual exploration and choice and fosters an intrinsic motivation. This kind of "autotelic" environment attempts to replicate the fundamentals of play; that is, there must be no serious consequences, and it must be fun. It also adds the element of inductive reasoning.

People are conceptualizing organisms. Given an intrinsically motivating, responsive learning situation they demonstrate enormous information-processing capacity. We see this in young children when they are placed in process environments allowing for make-believe play or responsive language acquisition (using the talking typewriter). As Moore himself has said, "By the time a child is three, he has achieved what is probably the most complex and difficult task of his lifetime—he has learned to speak. Nobody has instructed him in this skill; he has had to develop it unaided. . . . There's plenty of information processing ability in a mind that can do that."

3. The Inductive Teaching Program (ITP). The Inductive Teaching Program is a specialized means of transmitting information that differs from more traditional methods of teaching and learning in that it gives the student minimum structure and maximum degrees of freedom in the learning situation. Used in conjunction with a complex learning problem, it provides material to the student in a way that permits him to generate higher level plans or strategies for making decisions, based on the consideration and comparison of self-gathered units of information.

Specifically, the Inductive Teaching Program consists of a set of facts about a particular problem, situation, or academic subject, stored on individual cards, analogous to the memory storage banks utilized by computers. The student is charged with the responsibility of getting these facts by the "inquiry" method: asking questions that will solicit these pieces of information. Each fact is stored on an IBM punch card—typewritten on the blank side if the information is longer than 80 alphabetic characters, punched and interpreted (printed) on the front side if the information is 80 or fewer characters. (When computer facilities are not available the information can be placed on ordinary strips of paper or index cards. The reason for using punch cards—when available with computer hardware—is that such cards can be reproduced and processed more quickly.) The idea of developing "memory storage banks" with enough information units to answer almost any question posed by a student in a given situation has already been accomplished in several contexts (e.g., Karlins, 1967; Karlins, Coffman, Lamm, and Schroder, 1967; Karlins and Lamm, 1967; Karlins, Schroder, and Streufert, 1965).

In the Inductive Teaching Program the student is involved in every phase of the learning process—from his active information search and processing of requested information to his utilization of this information in decision making. Inductive teaching is similar to programmed learning in the sense that the student is allowed to control the rate at which information is received; it is different from programmed learning in that it makes the student active in the information-organization process. The Inductive Teaching Program can be summarized by its: (a) flexible teaching pattern: the student determines what will be taught (and when) by his pattern of information request; (b) flexible, responsive environment that provides feedback to the learner relevant to his inputs; (c) demands on the student for active manipulation of information; (d) emphasis on interactive connections between the student and the environment he is investigating; and (e) storage of *factual* material only.

The most important aspect of the Inductive Teaching Program is its emphasis on decision making through student-instigated inductive reasoning: the Inductive Teaching Program contains the basic units of information necessary for decision making; the learner is required to accumulate and process the information in self-meaningful and relevant ways for problem solving. The informational program deck (deck of answer cards to the students' questions) serves only as a repository of facts, it is not a storehouse of synthesized or creative problem solutions. In his questioning the student may, through information request, receive facts concerning the problem he is interested in—*but all assumptions, inferences, and extrapolations from these facts must be generated by the learner.* If Newton were learning via the Inductive Teaching Program he could, if he asked, receive the piece of information that "apples fall from the tree branches to the ground below"—but any postulation of a law of gravity from this information would be an induction and thus, of necessity, be constructed by Newton rather than the Inductive Teaching Program, which offers no such organization of the informational facts.

An example might bring the underlying philosophy behind the Inductive Teaching Program into sharper focus. In the Community Development Exercise, a complex problem-solving task utilizing the Inductive Teaching Program

(Karlins, 1967), students were required to find the best possible way to build a hospital, with the cooperation and aid of local natives, on the South Seas island of "Wabowa." As part of the solution to this problem the student might want to know the best location for building the hospital. There are two ways he could attempt to find an answer to his question: (a) he could send in a question card asking "where is the best place to build a hospital on Wabowa?"; (b) he might ask several questions related to the location problem (e.g., type, availability, and distribution of natural resources, terrain of the land, transportation facilities, population concentrations, labor supply, climatic conditions, land use and ownership, etc.); such information, when put together, will allow him to make a decision as to the best construction site. In the former case the student has asked an "inferential question" that requires a creative problem solution not available to him through the factual information contained in the Inductive Teaching Program. In the latter case the student has made the proper response: he has asked for factual information that can be used to arrive at the answer he seeks.

As a final example, the ITP might be viewed in relation to a teacher in a typical content-oriented classroom situation. In ordinary teacher-student interaction the instructor serves as both a disseminator of facts and an information-processing system. That is, sometimes the teacher presents factual information, other times conclusions and inferences based on factual information. In the ITP, the instructor retains his function of providing factual information to the student but relegates to the student the task of processing the information and drawing conclusions from it. It is now the student, not the teacher, who provides the framework for factual data, who builds his own structure of reality from the raw materials of factual information. No step of information processing is hidden from the student, for he must take every step by himself. The role of teacher as purveyor of factual material only is similar to that demanded of instructors in Suchman's (1961) inquiry training paradigm, where instructors are allowed to answer "yes" or "no" to factual questions posed by students. Inferential questions, however, are not answered.

The major requirement that must be fulfilled in the inductive teaching method is that the pool of information concerning a given problem or situation be extensive enough to provide suitable answers to the majority of any questions that might be asked by a child in his information request. The ultimate goal of the ITP is to be able to provide a factual answer to any properly posed question asked by a learner in his exploration of a given problem environment. Thus, whereas it is a student's job to explore a given environment through question asking so that he can acquire a sufficient body of facts to come to a conclusion, it is the responsibility of the ITP to provide an information-rich environment with enough answers to provide the student with the means of making such conclusions possible.

Composition of the Inductive Teaching Program and its use in a problem solving context: The Community Development Exercise (CODE). An example of how the ITP is embedded in a problem-solving task, to be utilized by the student in learning about the task and solving the problem, is evident in the Community Development Exercise, which required students to request and utilize information about a novel environment in solving a difficult problem. For the interested reader, a description of Inductive Teaching Programs and the Community Development Exercise is included in Appendix B and it is hoped that a study of same will lead to a better understanding of the development and function of Inductive Teaching Programs in general and the CODE Inductive Teaching Program in particular.

Measures built into the Inductive Teaching Program. At all stages of the decision-making process, measures are built into the Inductive Teaching Program to provide accurate assessment of the student's information-processing skills. A discussion of some of these measures can be found in Chapter 3 (pp. 36–42).

In the inductive teaching procedure the child is required to seek information about a specific problem or situation (by asking relevant questions) and then utilize this information to arrive at the best possible solution to the problem. In such a training procedure, the child learns how to search for information in his environment and how to put it together in new and meaningful ways in coping with the world. In the course of processing the information, the student is also *learning* the information—sometimes better than he might by content-oriented procedures. It is a well-documented educational finding that students learn material fastest and remember it longest when it is interesting and challenging. For instance, students who have taken the Community Development Exercise speak of their fascination with the problem and the procedure for solving it. They see the task as a worthy and enjoyable intellectual challenge—a chance to test their wits on a novel, unsolved problem.

As a learning device, the Inductive Teaching Program can be utilized in yet another way. In some less complex problems students working alone or in groups can be made responsible for creating various problem situations and their accompanying sets of information (Reactive Program Decks). It is an excellent way to encourage the child to learn about a given topic. It stands to reason that when an individual has researched a topic to the point that he can answer most of the questions someone else would ask about it—he has a competent knowledge of that topic.

PROCESS ENVIRONMENTS IN CURRENT EDUCATION

It would be a mistake to assume that contemporary educators have failed entirely to capitalize on the interest that process environments hold for students. Perhaps the natural scientists have been most cognizant of the value of process environments in education. Such men place great emphasis on the laboratory in which the child is supposedly required to explore, formulate questions, observe, generate hypotheses from such observations, make further observations, and so on. In the areas of physical education (sports) and the fine arts (dramatics), process education is also practiced on some occasions.

Unfortunately, most contemporary process education is not very effective the few times it is practiced. For instance, the natural science laboratory is, in actuality, often far from an ideal process environment. Learning often takes place by the "cookbook" method where students are required to memorize and mix some predetermined chemical "recipe"; followed by the careful observation of reactions the book has already enumerated. There is precious little room for individual initiative and information processing within such a system. The same is often true in physical education and drama. Sports can become a series of rigidly programmed exercises, plays called from the sidelines, and fixed courses of action to be memorized before the game (as witness Little League baseball). Student actors are many times forced to observe the rigid interpretations of their teacher-director in their roles; for example, "Never turn your back on the audience." Even in art classes, the child is frequently limited in the degree to which he can express his own creative urges. Too often the child learns that good art is art the teacher *thinks* is good. If the teacher likes geometric designs and Johnny likes flowers—Johnny had better well begin drawing parallelograms or else he receives little if any reinforcement.

Now it is true that some teachers are exceedingly skilled in creating effective process environments, but these individuals are in a minority. As everyone knows, gifted teachers are as rare as gifted scientists or gifted leaders. We cannot continue to rely upon the occasional emergence of such exceptional individuals to solve our problem. Most contemporary instructors simply do not have the skills and cannot draw upon the resources necessary to create the materials needed for process education to work. This is certainly not their fault. Such materials are not easy to develop and converting these educational goals into actual classroom operations requires a high degree of ingenuity. As we indicated earlier, we will need large scale organizations (institutes and corporations) to provide the teacher with the appropriate and validated materials to implement process-learning programs. Indeed, there are several such process "programs" already available (although many more, of course, will be needed); for example, *Science—A Process Approach; Man: A Course of Study; National Schools Project,* to name only three of the more extensive curricula that are well grounded in theory and research (applied as well as basic). These programs are carefully reviewed in Chapter 5 of H. P. Cole's vital work *Process Education: an Emerging Rational Position* (1970). At this point, however, we will be satisfied to reiterate our statement that the teacher is *not* to be blamed for the general scarcity of effective process-oriented educational environments in our schools. Until the necessary materials are made available to instructors throughout the school systems, until instructors are trained in their application, and *until the school systems come to accept and use these materials* (Chapter 6), process education must remain an aspiration rather than a reality.

When one takes the time to examine the process environments that have been tried in contemporary education, he is confronted by a surprising discovery: whereas the teaching methods we propose have been partially adopted in the physical sciences and in the fine arts, they have been almost totally absent from instruction in the "social" areas, such as social studies, civics, and history.[7] And it is precisely in these areas of *social* behavior that our citizenry is currently experiencing its most severe difficulties. We contend that it is in the social sciences that process education can be most effectively and beneficially employed. Further, in Chapter 5 we will provide examples of how process education might help relieve some of our social-political problems, such as racial prejudice.

In its most recent application, the Inductive Teaching Program (along with other components of a process environment) is being implemented in a large interdisciplinary program at Southern Illinois University under the direction of H. M. Schroder (1971). Like all other Inductive Teaching Programs it: (1) presents a problem for the individual to solve; (2) requires the individual to generate questions in solving the problem; (3) develops an individual's information-processing skills by his pattern of information search and organization; (4) is interesting and involving to the student; and (5) requires a set of answers that are relevant to the questions asked by the student.

CHARACTERISTICS OF ENVIRONMENTS FOR PROCESS LEARNING

What characterizes an "environment for process learning"? If we equip our teachers with the tools and philosophy of process education, and the educational system encourages their use, the following changes will be evidenced in our schools:

1. In School Policy. The basic requirement for determining curriculum will be that the materials included be *interesting* for the student. And almost any subject can meet such a requirement if it is made *relevant* for the learner.

When material is intrinsically interesting to the student—when he *wants* to learn it on its own merits—then extrinsic controls (antithetical to process learning) will *not* be necessary to accomplish such learning. A. S. Neill claims the primary goal of education is happiness for the child. Happiness to Neill means an interest in what one is doing. "I would rather have a happy street cleaner than a neurotic scholar" is the way Neill puts it. We agree.

To insure the student's interest in educational materials, he should be offered a choice of what he wants to learn. He may not choose to learn what some of his friends or teachers want him to choose, but as we indicated earlier, with practice, he will learn to modulate. When a child is forced to learn something he perceives as irrelevant and boring, he learns it only under the contingency of extrinsic force. At this point, the teacher is forced into the role of disciplinarian rather than instructor.

Progress toward a process-oriented education will necessitate a revision about our notion of a fixed set of "requirements" for all students. It is true that enforcement of such requirements does produce some students who are "good at everything." But the price of such "all-round" knowledge is high: the rise of extrinsic control and a lot of disinterested students. Certainly it is important that our students get a taste of what subjects there are to learn (thus some introduction to various curriculum topics is necessary)—but the current inflexibility and extent of curriculum requirements could be certainly reduced without a serious loss to the student's comprehension of what topics of study were available for learning.

In summary, then, for process education to be effective the schools must provide for the student the chance to learn subjects he wants to learn—subjects he perceives as relevant to his needs and interests. One way to make sure he chooses subjects that have been traditionally defined as "important" (e.g., math, science, and history) is to make these topics relevant to his interests.

2. In School Design. To accomplish process goals in education will require actual *architectural* changes in the school environment. (This point is being recognized by an ever-growing number of scholars—as witnessed by an issue of *Harvard Educational Review* (1969) devoted to the topic.) Today's teachers—no matter how able or motivated to implement process goals— will find the going nearly impossible in today's schools. As we emphasized earlier, classrooms with row upon row of desks facing the "pulpit" of the professor, do little to foster an atmosphere of free inquiry and joyful learning. It is true that when each child has his own desk TV monitor (which is not far off judging from current technological advances) he will have access to the diversity of information he will need for effective process learning in some domains—but even this innovation will not promote process learning in the social areas. One of the best ways for a child to learn about social processes —to appreciate and respect the views of others—is to participate in these processes through interaction with others. Schools need to provide facilities for social-studies laboratories—small rooms wired for video and audio feed-back where children can interact in task-oriented groups.

When classrooms are provided where students come together and learn from each other, process learning will be facilitated. Following a session where an individual has privately undertaken information search and recommended a course of action concerning a problem, he is excited about discovering the conceptualizations of others: how *they* went about solving the task and what conclusions they reached. One way to satisfy each student's interest in this matter and promote process learning at the same time is to bring small groups of students together to discuss their individual strategies for accomplishing the goal. In these group sessions, the child learns of the conceptions of others; comes to recognize that alternative conceptions of the problem are possible; and sees how different conceptions lead one to search for different types of information and arrive at different conclusions. In these sessions the student comes to value and respect differences in problem-solving strategies between individuals, and learns how to utilize such different approaches in his future information processing.

Thus far, efforts to set up "social-studies laboratories" have not always met with warm receptions. A proposal to set up a process-oriented social-studies laboratory, which was supported by an entire school district in New Jersey, was rejected by the Office of Education as having a low priority. The purpose of the proposal is still important and viable today: to design and build a mobile social-studies laboratory that can be moved from school to school to demonstrate the methods and value of process education in social studies. The cost of such a facility for a regular school district would be small. As a mobile facility it could service two or three schools in one area at the same time.[8]

3. In Class Materials. The books, tests, and other materials used in support of process-centered education should:

A. Be interesting to the student.

B. Permit the student to generate information through his own information search efforts and utilize this information in decision making (many of the tasks, topics, and activities can be developed and used instructionally by the students themselves).

C. Provide a responsive, changing environment in which the student can receive feedback relevant to his evolving problem-solving strategies.

D. Permit the student to move from information generation to conceptual organization, back to information generation, and so on. It is this movement from one process to another, from the generation of discrepant information to the combination of this information in problem solving that overcomes boredom and creates interest. We are in agreement with O.K. Moore who points out that it is not the amount of time spent on one topic (math, history, etc.) that produces boredom—it is the time spent before a discrepancy in information is provided or discovered.

E. Measure the degree of process learning independently of content learning (Chapter 3).

Under certain circumstances in class, materials can be produced by the students themselves. Such a case in point is the development of Reactive Program Decks for Inductive Teaching Programs (Chapter 3). Here students can research a topic and generate the answer cards that will be used to reply to the questions of their classmates.

PROCESS ENVIRONMENTS AND PROCESS LEARNING

Process environments are designed so that learning proceeds via the child's ability to generate alternative conceptualizations of information and use these conceptions in solving problems. Children who have had little experience in such an environment—that is, children who are accustomed to content learning and content-learning environments—would be expected to experience difficulty in coping with process environments.

From a developmental point of view, content learning predisposes one to look externally for rewards and guidelines, to seek a definitive answer to every problem, while avoiding ambiguity and conflicting information. All these characteristics reduce the child's capacity to profit from a process environment and, consequently, his process grades should be significantly lower than his content grades in school (assuming such grades will someday exist side by side).

David E. Hunt has conceptualized these interactions between teaching environment and information-processing level of the student in his work on matching models (Hunt, 1970). In one study (Tonlinson and Hunt, 1971) results indicate that students with low information-processing skills (presumably having less experience in process environments) performed comparatively better in a content than in a process environment, whereas the type of environment made little difference to students with well-developed information-processing ability.

To overcome a student's inability to deal effectively in a process environment, we must begin to place children in process-learning situations at an early age. It is in this effort where parental influences directed at process learning and the development of educational toys and headstart programs can be most beneficial.

SUMMARY

After briefly reviewing some of the problems associated with content-centered education some examples of process-learning environments are presented. These include "make believe play"; Moore and Anderson's "talking typewriter"; and the Inductive Teaching Program.

It is suggested that some process environments exist in current American education but that these are few in number and relatively ineffective. Such a state of affairs is not the teachers' fault. Until the necessary process materials and training in the use of process materials are made available to instructors throughout the school systems, and until the school systems come to accept and *use* these materials, process education must remain an aspiration rather than a reality. It is also pointed out that whereas process methods have been partially adopted in the physical sciences they have been almost totally absent from instruction in the "social" areas: social studies, history, civics, etc. Because it is in the domain of social behavior that the American is experiencing great difficulties, it is recommended that process education in the social sciences might well help the citizen overcome some of his problems in interpersonal relations.

The chapter concludes with a discussion of the changes that will have to take place in our schools if process-centered education is to be realized. These changes will involve *school policy, school design,* and *course materials.*

One of the consequences of process education is discussed: children who have had little experience in such an environment (who are accustomed to content learning and content-learning environments) would be expected to experience difficulty in coping with process-oriented problems. To overcome such a state of affairs, it is suggested that children be given experience in process-learning situations at an early age.

" ... Learning which makes a difference—in the individual's behavior, in the course of action he takes in the future, in his attitudes and in his personality ... not just an accretion of knowledge." Carl Rogers

5. Process Learning, Self, and Social Development

The noblest goal of the individual is to develop the capacity to be free, and the aim of all institutions and governments should be to help the individual in his quest for freedom. Individuals differ in their ability to be free. It is a *learned* ability—an information-processing ability—unrelated to the amount of knowledge a person learns or his memory capacity. Freedom is the ability of a person to produce his own conceptions, to generate alternative and conflicting conceptions, to think and value in terms of multiple perspectives, and to define one's identity and his relationships to others on the basis of these self-generated conceptions of the world.

We argue that much of contemporary education, with its emphasis on content learning, is frustrating a child's efforts to achieve a more mature concept of freedom which, in turn, inhibits his potential to live and work together harmoniously and constructively with others. If our capacity to be free is defined by information-processing ability, then the degree of process learning in schools and at home may well determine (or strongly influence) the form and nature of our social relationships and cultural institutions in the future.

THE RELATIONSHIP BETWEEN EDUCATION AND PERSONALITY

The common tendency to draw a sharp distinction between the development of personality and educational development is a logical outcome of adopting a "content" view of education. When we define and measure education by the amount of knowledge acquired, it is indeed relatively independent of what we generally understand as "personality." That is, the amount of formal knowledge acquired at school in subjects such as history, or literature, is known to be comparatively unimportant in shaping a person's concept of himself, his identity, his characteristic defense mechanism, and the way he interacts with others (e.g., the degree of hostility he expresses toward minority group members).

Yet, education does have a very definite impact on the personality development of the child. It helps shape the development of his outlook not by what is taught but *how* it is taught. People who point out that education and personality are not related, basing their argument on the discontinuity between formal knowledge and personal development, do not realize that school experiences also affect a child's information-processing ability—an ability that very definitely does play a role in personality development.

Today education has an ever-increasing influence in the developing personality of the child—whether educators realize it or not. From preschool on, children are placed in specified classroom environments and taught by specified instructional methods that shape their social and personal development by affecting the way they learn to think and perceive the world. In any educational setting—content or process centered—we must look beyond the information being learned to *how* the child is learning to process information if we wish to see the impact of education on personality development in the child. When we observe that education, by teaching the student a *way* of thinking, is influencing his self-concept, his conception of others, and his ability to adapt to the world, then we begin to understand the power of the school in shaping each pupil's personality.

EDUCATIONAL ENVIRONMENTS AND PERSONALITY DEVELOPMENT

In the traditional content-oriented home or school environment, the training agent (parent or teacher) gives the child a set of predetermined "rules" to live by and then rewards or punishes him based on the degree to which he follows these rules. In environments emphasizing content learning the child learns more than content. He also learns an extrinsic theory of control. He learns to adopt a "reactive" strategy—to look to others for guidelines for his actions and rewards for his efforts. Traditional theories of learning currently guiding educational policy focus on this aspect of the person as a *reacting* organism. To the reacting individual, feelings of worth and well-being arise when he achieves an understanding of what the training agent expects of him. The "desire" to behave as the training agent demands leads to patterns of dominance *and* submission in the child. This paradoxical state of affairs is well explained by Fromm (1941) who points out that patterns of dominance and submission result from the *same* adaptive strategy. When the child is instructed by traditional content-centered methods, he learns to experience insecurity and anxiety when he cannot respond according to the criteria that exists in the parents' or teachers' head. He is learning, in other words, to be *submissive* or to feel uncomfortable.

But at the same time that the child feels submissive to the training agent, he is also assimilating the rules of that agent and rigidly applying them in his behavior toward others. When the standards of other individuals conflict with the standards the child has learned via his training agent—or when other peoples' responses do not coincide or agree with the responses he has learned—anxiety occurs. To overcome this anxiety the child will often try to bring the behavior of others "into line" with the standards he has been taught. This is *dominant* behavior that serves the same generic purpose as submission.

In a content-oriented learning environment, the child is also learning to seek structure and certainty. Since judgments of self-worth are anchored in standards that are external to oneself, it is important for the content-trained individual to know these standards "cold"—to be absolutely sure of what they are and how they relate to his behavior. The rules or standards of the training agent become "absolutes"—behavioral programs to be followed at all costs, or rejected totally. Such an absolutistic strategy generates a very low level of information-processing skill in the practitioner: the individual learns to construe information in only one, rigid, unchanging way. As a result of such functioning, the child never learns to generate alternative conceptions, to create conflict and uncertainty for himself, to understand that opposing conceptions exist and must be jointly considered in decision making. And, of course, he never learns to *enjoy* and *seek* uncertainty and conflicting conceptions—activities that have been empirically related to productive thinking, problem solving, and creativity by investigators such as Berlyne and Guilford. Maslow (1962, 1970), in describing the *healthy* adult personality, has this to say about such individuals: "They do not cling to the familiar, nor is their quest for truth a catastrophic need for certainty, safety, definiteness and order . . . doubt, tentativeness, uncertainty, with the consequent necessity for abeyance of decision, which is for most a torture, can be for some a pleasantly stimulating challenge, a high spot in life rather than a low."

An overemphasis on the more extreme forms of content learning in the home, church, and school decreases conceptual maturity and increases the likelihood of authoritarian and/or antidemocratic elements in the personality. The adult authoritarian personality, according to Frenkel-Brunswik and others (Adorno, Frenkel-Brunswik et al., 1950), is a basic character structure that possesses certain interrelated characteristics: (1) a strong disposition to conform; that is, an exaggerated tendency to look to authority sources for approval or disapproval of one's behavior, beliefs, and emotions; (2) a high degree of rigidity and resistance to change along with a fierce loyalty to the values of the in-group; (3) a fear or intolerance of differences or conflict; (4) a need for pat solutions and an intolerance of ambiguity; (5) in interpersonal relationships, a heavy emphasis on power and status; and (6) excessive use of the defense mechanisms of displacement and projection (e.g., "projecting" an unacceptable feeling about oneself, such as cruelty, as characteristic of other people rather than of one's self). Furthermore, it was postulated that the roots of this type of personality syndrome lay in early child-training practices. That is to say, that rigid poles of control (on the part of the parent) and submission (on the part of the child) in the family organization, and the inculcation of absolute ("correct") attitudes and behaviors lay the groundwork for the development of an authoritarian personality and for prejudice.

In process-learning environments, the constraint of seeking rewards by striving to comply to external standards is removed. In its place, the child gains feelings of self-worth through exploration, concept formation, and conception organization and utilization in decision making. The focus is on the intrinsic, proactive (as opposed to extrinsic-reaction) process. The child is generating his own ideas, forming concepts from various points of view, and considering their relevance in making judgments. In this environment, the child is learning to develop internal control (self-responsibility) and standards. Such intrinsic standards are flexible rather than brittle, complex rather than simple, and continually undergoing change in response to changing environmental demands.

CONCEPTUAL MATURITY AS A FACTOR IN INTERPERSONAL RELATIONS

Just as the degree of conceptual maturity (level of information-processing ability) can be measured as a "process grade" in a particular school subject such as social studies or history, it can also be measured in the domain of interpersonal relations. Following a course in social studies or some aspects of the American Indian, for example, the process grade could be based on the student's ability to generate a number of relevant concepts about these Indians in a certain situation and his capacity to use these different conceptions in solving a problem involving the Indians. Similarly, at any point in time we can measure a person's conceptual level (maturity) in the realm of interpersonal relations—for instance, how well he can cope with other individuals. Again, the process score a person receives will depend on the amount of process learning he has been exposed to at home and in school.

A process-scoring manual has been developed to assess conceptual maturity (information-processing ability) from sentence and paragraph completions (Schroder, Driver, and Streufert, 1967; Phares and Schroder, 1969). In this method, a trained rater is instructed to score subjects' responses to sentence stems (e.g., "When I am in doubt . . ." "When others criticize me it usually means . . .") in terms of the number of concepts utilized to generate the response. In other words, the rater is trained to ask: "What level of information-processing skill was necessary to generate this response?" The rater is trained to ignore the *content* of the response and to measure the *process* underlying it. The sentence-stem items are geared to be particularly relevant for interpersonal behavior in social and group task-oriented activities. Once the rater has learned the operations for scoring process skills, he can use those same operations to score any verbal or behavioral response in terms of how conceptually mature the response was (the level of information-processing skills needed to generate the answer).

A host of experimental studies have repeatedly demonstrated the importance of conceptual level in the realm of interpersonal relations. Persons with high scores on the conceptual maturity test—those, in other words, with well-developed information-processing skills—in comparison with individuals scoring lower on the test:

1. *Explore and/or discover more diverse and relevant information about people in group settings* (Driver, 1962; Lee, 1968; Stager, 1966).

2. *Generate more conceptions of a problem situation, interrelate these conceptions more often, and arrive at better (more adaptive) decisions in group settings* (Streufert and Schroder, 1965; Streufert, 1962, 1966). Low conceptual-level persons, when working together, typically arrive (by consensus) at a single conception of a problem and use this unitary point of view exclusively in their information search and decision making in the problem-solving environment. Mildly discrepant feedback from the problem environment—information not in agreement with the group's conception of the situation—is often distorted to fit into the conception already agreed upon. Only highly conflicting feedback can affect the group's conception about the problem environment, at which point the conception is modified to encompass the new data and again utilized as an exclusive, rigid way of viewing the ongoing situation. Such strategy is alright if the problem environment is relatively static. But few such environments exist. Most problem situations are constantly changing and, consequently, single conception thinking (even when modified fairly regularly) becomes ineffective in dealing with a changing, dynamic situation. It seems that such a cognitive approach is always "lagging behind" the unfolding problem—suggesting solutions that are "dated" efforts two or three steps behind the times.

Conceptually mature persons working together generate more than a single conception of a problem when alternative conceptions are relevant. Such alternative approaches might represent different hypotheses about a situation—for example, different ways to construe information in a war game or an internation simulation. Different conceptions can also be generated from the enemy's (or opponent's) point of view—for example, in terms of their long and short term goals. Groups composed of conceptually mature individuals search for information and make decisions on the basis of a number of relevant conceptions—a strategy that provides maximum flexibility, optimal use of information, and is less likely to lead to decisions irrelevant to the current state of affairs.

An individual with fewer and/or less well-integrated concepts about other persons is more likely to evaluate others as either very good or very bad (Coffman, 1967). That is, evaluations of people based on a unitary conception are more likely to be extreme than evaluations emerging from the organization of two or more conceptions. For most individuals, then, overall evaluations based on multiple integrated concepts will be less extreme than those formulated on the basis of fewer, less well-integrated concepts because negative conceptions will be balanced by other more positive concepts generating more moderate evaluations.

The net effect of low information-processing ability in human relations is for the conceptually immature individual to increase the psychological distance between himself and persons he perceives as "different" from him. In a threatening situation, such psychological distances increase rapidly and the chances of hostile actions are enhanced. The reason for this state of affairs is that the conceptually immature individual has not generated a number of different conceptions about other persons. Thus, in the case of threat, negative affect grows rapidly in him because he has no alternative inputs about the offending person (or group) to check his anger (Tomkins, 1963).

While we may define prejudice as an overgeneralized negative or hostile attitude toward a specified group of people, it seems clear to us that conceptual immaturity in dealing with humans is the foundation of that prejudice. The level of conceptual maturity determines an individual's potential for prejudice. Concerning prejudice, it is interesting to note that just because a person possesses a positive attitude toward some people (or groups of people) does not guarantee an absence of hostile, prejudicial attitudes toward other individuals or groups, or that he will not develop such prejudicial attitudes given appropriate conditions.

When members of a group challenge a person's own beliefs or threaten him in some way, negative conceptions toward that offending group emerge. The more immature the conceptual development of the individual, the more rapidly intensely negative conceptions arise in such an instance. This is unfortunate, for the expression of prejudice further reduces the possibility of developing alternate conceptions toward the offending party or group in question.

It is also important to realize—in keeping with psychoanalytic theory—that an offending individual or group does not actually have to disconfirm an individual's expectations or attitudes to threaten him. Should a person low in conceptual maturity become insecure, for whatever reasons, he has the tendency to blame others for his dilemma (the phenomenon of "scapegoating")—seeing the "other guy" as a threat to his well being.

Although we believe that a person's level of conceptual development determines his potential for being prejudiced, we also recognize that there are conditions under which even conceptually mature individuals will exhibit prejudicial behaviors. This is true because prejudice is an outcome of the interaction between conceptual maturity and the social conditions or norms prevalent at any one time. In some cultures where the external pressures and supports for prejudice are very strong (as in South Africa or sections of the southern United States), persons will express prejudice regardless of their conceptual maturity. In other areas where external pressures are weaker, it is the conceptually immature individuals who will be primarily involved in expressing prejudice.

THE SCHOOL AND CONCEPTUAL MATURITY IN HUMAN RELATIONS

What is the role of education in reducing racial prejudice in our society? Recent studies indicate that prejudice is reduced if black and white groups, in equal status, share a common goal or fate and are interdependent upon each other to achieve that goal (i.e., the individuals need each other in order to solve the problem or achieve the goal) (Ashmore, 1969, 1970; Brunstein and McCrae, 1962; Fesbach and Singer, 1957; Mann, 1959; Singer, 1969; Sherif and Sherif, 1953; Sherif, 1958; Allport, 1954, Williams, 1964). It is important here to note that for different individuals or groups merely to co-exist near each other does not, in and of itself, necessarily reduce prejudice nor will a single kind of experience, in isolation, permanently erase the negative attitude. The interaction must take place on a continuing, common-goal basis.

Presumably, when people interact on a continuing, "even basis," greater opportunity is provided for both sides (e.g., blacks and whites) to develop and use conceptions of each other. They can learn to put themselves in the other fellow's shoes more easily and come to understand his perspectives in social interaction. The ability to comprehend and utilize these perspectives of others in interpersonal relations lies at the very heart of mature conceptual functioning (and thus at the heart of reducing racial prejudice).[9]

Given this information, let us return to our question: What role does education play in eliminating racial prejudice in our country? The schools, due to the Supreme Court desegregation ruling of 1954, offers the best (possibly the only) environment where black and white children can undertake equal-status interaction in solving meaningful problems! The home, so effectively segregated by races in most communities, offers little hope of meaningful face-to-face interaction between white and black children.

Let us present some ways that the educational system could be utilized to reduce racial prejudice in our country. One effective national program in our schools that could produce reductions in prejudice in a relatively short period of time would involve the introduction of process education in social-studies classes. This program would focus on process materials and procedures specifically developed to build conceptual maturity in interpersonal and intergroup relations. Already, curricula for the development of such programs are available (e.g., Sefarian and Cole, 1972). Programs could also be developed in athletics (if the competition for leadership and status in the group does not replace the overall cooperative goal) and drama, but these areas are usually limited to a few talented students.

In this process-education program, conceptual development in human relations would be enhanced by utilizing procedures that engage small groups of black and white students in meaningful interaction in the pursuit of superordinate goals that: (1) cannot be achieved by any child without the support and cooperation of other group members, and (2) cannot be meaningfully solved without taking both black and white students' perspectives into account. The value and power of superordinate goals in reducing intergroup tensions and prejudice have already been imaginatively and powerfully demonstrated by Sherif and Sherif (1953) in their pioneering work, *Groups in Harmony and Tension.*

The development of process tasks that are intrinsically interesting to children, have some effect on their lives, and involve them all in finding solutions relevant to a given problem are not easy to create. But we know the requirements each process task must meet if it is to be successful in reducing racial prejudice—the only problem facing us is the utilization of our imagination to create such tasks.

One such procedure, which has just been successfully tested (Gardiner, 1971), utilized a job-evaluation task as a training vehicle. Adolescent white students were given a description of two roles that would be played by a person who had to perform the job in question, for example, a class president whose job would entail, among other things, competence in the roles of social leader and decision maker. The students were also given three conceptual dimensions ("personal qualities"), such as extroversion and patience, which were deemed relevant to the task; but were asked to list as many other qualities as they felt were important to performance on the job. The purpose of this phase of training was to insure that the job evaluation would be based on adequate and relevant information. In other words, the purpose was to increase the subject's differentiation, thus establishing a basis for the formation of informationally rich concepts.

After familiarizing themselves with this material, the students next watched prepared videotaped interviews of four different people who were ostensibly candidates for the job of class president. Two candidates or "stimulus persons" were young blacks, and the other two young whites. Although the students were not aware of the fact, these taped interviews had been carefully structured and rehearsed so that one of the black candidates and one of the white candidates were approximately equally qualified on the various qualities that had been designated as relevant to the components of the job. While the student was watching the videotaped interviews, he rated the person being interviewed on all the qualities that had been supplied or that he had listed in his "Psychological evaluation booklet."

The first interview watched by the students was one involving a relatively bland and somewhat neutral white stimulus person. During this interview, the subjects were given rather detailed instructions as to how they were to carry out the evaluation task, and were thoroughly acquainted with the mechanics of the experimental procedure. This intensive aspect of training was designed to initiate high-level conceptual processes in the absence of threatening stimuli. Had the students been immediately exposed to the videotape of the highly competent black stimulus person, they might have reacted with a certain amount of hostility or anxiety (prejudiced persons are subject to sudden, acute attacks of anxiety), and it has been well established that anxiety has the effect of reducing thinking to a simplistic level. In short, presenting the "black competent" videotape immediately might have effectively destroyed the impact of the training procedure. Gardiner's subjects were exposed to the more threatening material only after they had evaluated three relatively inoffensive videotaped interviews, and after high-level conceptual processes had been safely established.

In the main training procedure itself, after the students had watched a videotaped interview and rated the stimulus person on all of the personal qualities, they would then form two "concepts" of the person—one of the person as a social leader, and another of the person as a decision maker. That is, each student was asked to visualize how the ostensible candidate would behave in each of the two roles. Each subject was urged to keep in mind, and organize into a unified impression, all of the ratings that he had given the stimulus person on the personal qualities listed in his booklet; but he was also encouraged to form a *different* impression or concept of the stimulus person in each role. This stage of forming different, alternative impressions is of criticaı importance in training students in multiconceptual thinking about racial affairs.

Once the subjects had formed alternative concepts of the stimulus persons, they were asked to rate how effective they thought each person would be in each of the two roles, and were finally asked to choose one videotaped person as class president. Following this, each student viewed two entirely new videotapes of two unfamiliar stimulus persons (one white and one black in that order) and proceeded to evaluate these persons as candidates for an unfamiliar job—school ombudsman. The purpose of this final phase of training was to generalize the complexity of the subject's thinking, and encourage him to develop his own conceptual dimensions and unified impressions. This latter goal was achieved by asking the subject to generate, on his own, all of the qualities relevant to the job of ombudsman, and to define for himself the different roles an ombudsman might have to play.

In addition to this main multiconceptual training procedure, a single-concept training condition was used in which a different group of students was required to form only one concept of each stimulus person, that is, they formed a concept of the stimulus person in the role of decision maker but not in the role of social leader. In every other respect, however, the single-concept procedure was identical to the multiconceptual procedure. Lastly, a control group of students was given an opportunity to view all of the videotaped interviews, but this control group was given no concept training of any sort.

Results of the Gardiner study indicated that both types of concept training were effective in reducing prejudice (on two separate measures of prejudice), but that the multiconceptual procedure was more effective than single-concept training. The control group, interestingly enough, showed no change in prejudice as a result of exposure to the videotapes. Although the multiconceptual training group showed greater prejudice reduction than the single-concept group, analysis of individual results revealed that subjects whose general conceptual level was low, benefited *more* from single concept training than from multiconceptual training. This finding is of great developmental significance, for it indicates that the development of process ability must take place gradually, with the difficulty of training being increased in a series of carefully graduated steps as the conceptual ability of the individual increases. In his recent book, Dr. David E. Hunt (1970) has discussed this notion in some detail under the label of "matching models in education." And in a related series of studies, Kohlberg has had considerable success in raising subjects' levels of moral understanding by graduating the training sequence and matching the difficulty of training to the individual's level of development.

An interesting follow-up to Gardiner's study might be to utilize group processes after concept training in order to bring about even further prejudice reduction. This could be achieved by having racially mixed, trained groups of subjects meeting together to discuss all aspects of the evaluation procedure and to arrive at a group choice for the job under consideration. Such interaction, if carried out on the basis of cooperative and task-oriented work necessitating equal status of all group members, could act as strong reinforcement for the complexity training procedure as well as promoting anxiety release and hostility reduction. A major problem in integrated classroom settings has been the general lack of meaningful procedures for bringing students of different races together, particularly immediately after integration has occurred when anxiety levels are extremely high, and when even minor misunderstandings can become major confrontations. Once such a confrontation has occurred, of course, it has a classic vicious-cycle property: anxiety is driven to a very high level, making further confrontations even more likely, which, in turn, leads to increased prejudice.

Another avenue for reducing prejudice is through meaningful student participation in the ongoing education process. By working together on projects relevant to their education, students become more involved with each other and their schooling. Today, students are basically passive in the school environment. They must be given real opportunity to make decisions that affect their educational lives—decisions such as: (1) teacher evaluation; (2) course and curriculum evaluation; (3) supervision of various school functions; and (4) disciplinary actions based on a student judicial system.[10]

In attempting to create process procedures designed to reduce racial prejudice, the need for the careful testing of all these procedures cannot be overemphasized. This is particularly true since shelves of books are full of ineffective and untested process materials.

SUMMARY

Three major topics were discussed in the chapter. In the section on *the relationship between education and personality,* it was emphasized that educational training does have a definite impact on a child's personality development not by what is taught but how it is taught. We argued that much of contemporary education, with its emphasis on content learning, is frustrating a child's efforts to achieve a more mature concept of freedom which, in turn, inhibits his potential to live and work together harmoniously and constructively with others. The way in which content-centered education creates authoritarian, externally controlled behavior in the individual was discussed.

In the second section, *conceptual maturity as a factor in interpersonal relations,* the importance of information processing skills in human interaction was stressed. It was pointed out that conceptually mature persons (in comparison to individuals less mature): (1) explore and/or discover more diverse and relevant information about people in group settings; (2) generate more conceptions of a problem situation, interrelate these conceptions more often, and arrive at better (more adaptive) decisions in group settings; (3) function at a more adaptive level under stress in group settings; (4) when interacting with others, are better able to perceive the world from another person's point of view and are better able to understand the impact of their behavior on other people and vice versa; (5) when placed together in groups for long periods of time, tend to form more democratic group organizations. It was suggested that such differences indicate that an individual's level of conceptual development in the interpersonal area has important implications for society: for its development as an intrinsic, democratic system; for its creative potential; and for the harmony of its interpersonal and intergroup relations.

In the concluding section of the chapter, the relationship between *conceptual maturity and the potential for prejudice* was described. It was hypothesized that the lower the level of conceptual maturity in the individual, the higher his potential for racial prejudice. The reasons for this hypothesis were presented along with a discussion of how the schools, utilizing process-learning procedures, could be utilized to reduce racial prejudice in America.

"The existing business of education as practiced in countless schools is not primarily concerned with learning. It is concerned with . . . maintaining institutions called schools. It is assumed that if schools are maintained, the education of the pupil will occur. This is a most doubtful assumption." H. P. Cole

6. Organizational Development in Education

Throughout our discussion we have argued that American education has failed to develop in our children the mature concept of freedom and responsibility necessary for living effectively in a complex, rapidly changing, democratic society. This state of affairs has come about in large measure because our teachers are not provided with the appropriate schools, training, materials, and tests needed to implement process learning. An even more basic factor that constricts our educational perspectives and practices to content-centered learning is the nature of educational organization that determines and regulates educational policy and practices. Too often, serious attempts to introduce process education into schools have been doomed because such a philosophy is incongruous with the goals of the entrenched, content-oriented organization that oversees American pedagogical procedures.

We assert that movement toward process goals in education will require organizational change and development in the administrative levels of our school systems. The nature of such changes will vary depending on the school system in question, its size, characteristics, needs and location. But certain principles, derived from information-processing theory and applicable to *all* schools, do provide guidelines for determining which changes must take place if we are to move toward a process-oriented educational system. A presentation of these guidelines, and suggestions for how they may be followed, will occupy us in this chapter. Developing a procedure for achieving organizational change will not be easy, but it is necessary if educational reform is to be successful.

CONTENT ORIENTATION AND EDUCATIONAL ORGANIZATION

In earlier chapters, we have shown how an extreme emphasis on content learning reduces the child's ability to "think for himself" in education and fosters an extrinsic system of rewards and punishments for controlling his behavior. Both these conditions reduce the development of constructive democratic processes in the school, on the playground, and throughout the community.

Actually, when content learning is the major goal of education, the whole school system takes on the characteristics of the content method. Moving up the educational hierarchy from student to teacher, we find the same directives at work: teachers are given prepackaged information by administrators and told how many days, hours, or minutes each child has to spend on each topic, which books and materials are to be used, and which tests are to be given. These instructors are expected, in turn, to pass on the prepackaged information to their students in the same autocratic manner: giving them a specified period of time to learn a specified amount of information, and so on.

In such a system, it is a testimony to the dedication and excellence of our teachers that they continue to work hard and to innovate as much as they do within the constricted latitude of freedom supplied in a content-centered system. Such an educational environment acts to dry up creativity and ingenuity on the part of teachers and students alike, depriving both instructor and pupil of choice, interest, and commitment; leaving instead a situation in which all control must be external. The student is moved to work out of a fear of failure or the external expectation of praise from teachers or parents, the teacher's efforts are spurred by power-wielding administrators who determine educational directives and reinforce conformity to those directives with their own "report cards" (e.g., job tenure and pay raises), while the administrators often feel themselves charged by the public to maintain the status quo or are flagellated for not correcting the system's errors and weaknesses (witness the recent statistics on job turnover of public school superintendents).

In such an educational system, communications and relations between the various educational participants—administrators, teachers, parents, students—are often weak, fraught with stress, and plagued with suspicion and distrust. In such a climate, it often seems as if parts of the educational system were coming undone, with no consensus of direction achieved between parents, students, civic groups, teachers, and administrators on educational procedures and goals. Each party to the educational process becomes, too often, a party unto itself—with no overall lines of communication and trust to bring it together with other parties in pursuit of educational reform.

In many ways, the content-oriented school organization functions in a manner similar to the students trained in such a system. By this we mean that *the content-centered educational organization functions as a unit much as a student with low information-processing skills functions as an individual.* Let's see how:

An individual with *mature* information processing skills is capable of considering many points of view (even when they conflict) in his problem solving. An effective information-processing organization does likewise. All organizations are formed to achieve goals that one or a few men cannot reach alone. An effectively functioning educational organization would make full use of each of its parts or units (administration, teachers, students, civic groups) to achieve an optimal educational system. It would consider the perspectives of these various groups in setting educational policy and objectives. An effectively functioning organization would also regularly measure the effects of its policies and utilize the findings in determining the future course of such policies. Thus, educational policy would not be considered sacrosanct, but rather, a flexible guideline for education—a guideline that would be changed with changing conditions. This is the way an *effectively* functioning educational organization would and should operate. It would be a flexible, unified educational organization performing on the basis of feedback from what it learns from all participant groups in the educational process.

Such an idealized, effectively functioning educational organization (proceeding in a manner reminiscent of the conceptually mature individual) is a far cry from the content-oriented educational organization we sketched earlier in which the various parties to the educational process are isolated, with policy makers having no way to bring the parties together and make use of their various perspectives in forging a viable, modifiable, realistic school program.

Now, one should not take the foregoing comments to mean that functional groups (e.g., teachers), should refrain from forming organizations aimed at achieving their own goals—indeed, these types of groups are essential. For it is only through such "interest groups" that the perspectives of teachers, for instance, can be heard, and where the teacher can establish standards of excellence for the profession and perhaps in the long run bring about process goals in education. What the foregoing comments *do* mean, however, is that when an organization becomes rigid and sluggish—as our current content-centered educational organizations seem to be—the functional parts have little effect on each other. Various educational groups do not engage in meaningful interaction and do not receive pertinent feedback from each other; nor do they work closely and harmoniously with administrative policy makers in defining and continually modifying educational policy and measurable objectives based on that policy.

POLICY CHANGE ATTEMPTS BY THE CURRENT EDUCATIONAL ORGANIZATION

Most of our present-day school organizations, in practice, are bureaucratic and hierarchical. Thus, the school organization exhibits those characteristics common to any bureaucracy: maintenance of its continued existence, resistance to change, fixed rules regarding the behavior of the participants and the roles they fill in the system, solidification of the communication channels between its parts, rewards for the participants who comply with and fulfill their assigned role expectations. Any human social system, of course, must provide a basic climate of stability in order to achieve its goal. In the case of the school, this goal is to provide meaningful learning for the child. However, when the stability becomes the end result, when it replaces the original goal (which is what so often happens in the bureaucratization process), the system then becomes dysfunctional. So we find that in these bureaucratic, hierarchical institutions the most common solution to problems is the application of *more* of what the organization already does; that is, in contemporary education, more content learning is prescribed. Since the organization does not have the potential to modify itself or its goals, it is only capable of generating the same old answers to the same old problems, even though such answers might be intensifying the existing crisis! Consequently, we continue to hear such stereotyped solutions to our current school difficulties as more of the same type of educational institutions, more required subjects in the curriculum, more workbooks with more prepackaged ideas, more hours of content learning, more teachers for fewer children, and so on. But all of these fixed "solutions" are content-oriented solutions—an application of the wrong medicine for our educational ills. Such "solutions" serve to maintain the system as it is and to accelerate and intensify the problems of content learning: an educational system that is rigid and fragmented into isolated groups of teachers, students, parents and administrators, and classrooms full of pupils with undeveloped information-processing skills. These problems severely retard both organizational as well as student efforts to be flexible and free in a rapidly changing society.

Because of the condition of contemporary educational organization, innovations in process learning (when they are introduced by progressive administrators or teachers) are difficult indeed to implement in today's school systems. Such will always be the case as long as the operational goals, values, and roles of the school system conflict with the goals, values and roles for process education (Cole, 1970, Chapter 3). Consider, for example, the results of two attempts to introduce changes into American classrooms:

1. One recent approach to reform within the current educational structure has been the development of summer institutes where teachers meet with "teacher trainers" and other "experts" to discuss pedagogical innovations in instruction and curriculum. Many of these institutes were established at universities, and most were far removed from the organizational restraints

of the typical classroom. Some institutes went so far as to introduce teachers to process-learning procedures, providing them with materials and training to implement process goals in the classroom (e.g., Time, Space and Matter; Madison Project). But, despite the well-meaning efforts of those involved, the summer institutes have met with little success primarily because they fail to take account of the organizational rigidity in the average school system. Such rigidity makes process procedures impossible to implant in the classroom. The teachers who had been trained at the institutes found this out soon enough. When they returned to their schools in the fall, anxious to try out the process methods they had mastered, they soon discovered that the demands of getting the student prepared to pass content-oriented examinations were more than enough to discourage any process learning! It was not long before the teacher was forced back into the content-centered approach in the classroom.

2. Another educational reform that is becoming more common involves the allotment of time during the school year for teachers to develop better instructional procedures and methods. Certainly the teacher must have ample time— perhaps one third of his working hours—outside of the classroom to prepare his lesson plans and to master new educational materials and procedures. But the reforms that allow him this much needed time are not that valuable for the implementation of process learning because the teacher does not have the materials and tests necessary to utilize process methods in his classes. Nor can the teacher be expected to develop or produce these materials and tests in his time outside the classroom. As we saw in Chapter 4, the development of process materials is a major undertaking that requires the full time skills of specially trained individuals. Instead of placing such an impossible onus upon the teacher, special scientific institutes or supporting services should be given the responsibility of creating process materials.

Even if we assume, however, that the teacher did have access to process materials (and could spend enough hours out of class to select and to prepare process-learning procedures), this would not guarantee the success of process learning in the schools. Why? Because unless an educational administration changes its philosophy to encompass process goals in the schools, merely giving the individual teacher more time during the academic year to work process learning into his teaching schedule will meet the same unsuccessful end as experienced by those instructors who attended summer institutes.

The problem with most contemporary innovators in education—no matter how well meaning they might be—is that they place the cart before the horse: *they try to introduce process education into a system which is not organized or ready to receive it.* As one administrator in a large public school system has stated, ". . . despite curricular innovations, some ideas about organizational change within the school, and some minor flirting with architectural design and TV, the basic contour lines of the public schools have remained remarkably untouched." The same observation has been made by other observers of the American educational system; for instance, Lippitt (1964):

"Our research is now rich with examples of opportunities provided but nothing gained, with new curricula developed but lack of meaningful utilization, with new teaching practices invented, with new, richer school environments but no improvement in the learning experience of the child." If process learning is to survive and flourish in America, we must modify educational organization to a point where it is capable of implementing process goals in our schools.

THE IMPLEMENTATION OF PROCESS-EDUCATIONAL GOALS IN THE AMERICAN SCHOOL SYSTEM

The changes that will be necessary to bring about process learning in the schools have been described earlier, but will be summarized here to focus on the *organizational* problem in achieving these changes. To create an atmosphere conducive to process learning, organized education will have to:

1. Develop and utilize additional criteria (or goals) against which it can judge its effectiveness—namely, *process* criteria (degree of information search, multiple-concept formation, self-instruction, etc.).

2. Provide materials that are *interesting* (relevant) to the student. This means that different children will be working in different educational subjects, depending on their interests and predilections.

3. Provide materials that encourage process as well as content learning.

4. Encourage institutes or internal divisions of curriculum development to create and evaluate effective and appropriate process materials and tests and provide supporting services to assist teachers.

5. Provide increasing opportunities for students to work on societal problems in an informationally rich environment and participate in small group learning experiences.

6. Develop procedures for handling individual differences in students' choices of topics and rates of progress in process learning.

7. Develop procedures for handling individual differences in instructors' process-teaching skills and approaches.

8. Stop viewing the teacher as a passive "distributor" or "disperser" of "ready-made" information. Regard the instructor as a person concerned with the management of a child's educational environment—as one who is responsible for giving the student encouragement to: (a) take an increasing role in his own education; (b) explore his world; (c) participate in group learning experiences; (d) develop his own values, and (e) strengthen his content and process skills. Such a shift in role should lessen considerably the conflict experienced by many teachers (particularly those newly entering the profession) who are child-centered but, because of the system's orientation, are forced into a role that services institutional needs.

9. Effect architectural changes in the school environment, moving from a "lecture-hall" design to classrooms that encourage student-student and student-teacher interaction.

10. Recognize that the initiation of process goals requires the involvement of all parts of the educational system (teachers, students, parents, and administrators) working cooperatively. The pursuit of process goals will lead to actual changes in the educational organization itself as well as in the roles of the various groups within the organization. Increasingly, the teacher will become a prime source of information for helping educational administrators determine what kinds of change should occur in the ongoing educational system. The teacher's role vis-a-vis the student will be that of a professional who specializes in the presentation of appropriate learning environments for optimal individual development. In cooperation with the school administrators, the teacher will provide educational environments to his students that are conducive to process learning.

11. Find acceptable ways to use classroom "technicians" whose task will be the operation of the many process materials utilized in the classroom (the need for these technicians will vary with the complexity and amount of process materials being utilized in any particular class). These technicians need not be regular teachers—they could, in fact, be individuals with high-school degrees or apprentices who have been trained in handling process materials. Their relationship to the teacher in the classroom is somewhat analogous to the interaction between orderlies and doctors in a hospital setting.

12. Develop methods for "quality checks" on the various process-learning materials, discarding those that are ineffective.

If these are some of the efforts organized education must make to create an atmosphere conducive to process learning, how can they best be accomplished?

PROCESS CRITERIA AND ORGANIZATIONAL DEVELOPMENT

Significant change in current educational practices can only be accomplished when the organization responsible for educational policy develops to a point where it can be responsive to the needs of the students and the demands of the society. Actual developmental change in educational organization has to occur *before* effective process learning can be realized. Without such organizational development, the various functioning parts of the educational system—teachers, students, parents, and administrators—cannot interact effectively and benefit from each other's experiences. *Such interaction is a prerequisite to the implementation of a successful process-learning program in our schools.*

In the last decade, much of the authors' research has focused on organizational factors underlying adaptive group and intergroup functioning—the type of functioning that will be necessary in the American educational organization if we hope to realize process learning in our schools (Schroder and Harvey, 1963; Driver, 1962; Streufert and Driver, 1966; Tuckman, 1964; Kennedy, 1962; Stager, 1966; Crouse, Karlins and Schroder, 1968; Phares and Schroder, 1969; Armitage, 1970). By putting together findings from our investigations with those of other researchers studying companies and educational systems (e.g., Roethlisberger, 1956; Likert, 1961, 1967; Cole, 1970; Havelock, 1969, 1970; Schmuck, 1968; Miles, 1967, etc.) we have come up with some changes we believe must be made in educational organization if process learning is ever to become a pedagogical reality.

STEPS IN THE IMPLEMENTATION OF PROCESS LEARNING IN OUR SCHOOLS

It is relatively easy for educators to specify, develop, and measure the effectiveness of various school objectives. It is an entirely different and more difficult task to change the educational organization so it can accomplish these objectives. An analogous problem is confronted by dieters: it is relatively simple for the overweight person to specify, develop, and measure his dieting objectives; it is another matter, however, for him to change his eating habits to realize those objectives!

Achieving effective organizational change and development involves a number of steps and procedures that are outlined in detail in a paper entitled, "The Measurement and Development of Management Information System," by H. M. Schroder (1970). The steps include diagnosis of current organizational procedures; setting up appropriate in-service training and planning procedures; implementation; follow-up and evaluation.

The nature of the plans and implementation will vary across school districts. In general, however, the organizational changes that would facilitate process orientations would include the following:

1. Increased Local and Teacher Responsibility. In the process-oriented educational system, the teacher—not the administrator—becomes the central decision-making figure concerned with the child's educational development. The goal of the teacher is to create in each student an intrinsic interest in education that will serve as the motivating force behind process and content learning alike. For the teacher to accomplish this challenging goal, he must be provided with new skills, educational services, curriculum flexibility, and relationships with school administrators.

Obviously, such an organizational "overhaul" that emphasizes a new role for the teacher and the principal, and a new criterion for education, cannot be achieved overnight. Organizational plans must go at a pace that ensures a smooth changeover from an administrative-centered educational system to a more open, responsive one, while not disrupting the ongoing learning process. The development of plans for inducing appropriate short and long term organizational change in education must involve all participating groups in the American school system: administrators, principals, teachers, representatives of various educational services, students, parents, school boards, and other relevant community policy makers.

2. Development of a "Service" and "Quality-Control" Orientation for Central Administration. There are obvious advantages inherent in a fairly large school system (e.g., 100 schools), particularly as teacher responsibility increases. Aside from factors such as the streamlining of purchasing and transportation, a particular size is required for a district to support and deliver effective services to teachers. As teachers increase their scope of responsibility, they will require information about alternative sets of materials, objectives, special training needed for staff, evaluations, costs, assistance in planning, and so on. In a more open and responsive system, the need for this kind of quality control increases. This is a central office function concerning the preparation of guidelines in all subject areas, and the assessment of levels of process and content criteria reached in various schools.

3. The Development of "Integrating" Groups. One of the chief factors facilitating organizational development is the establishment of continuing face-to-face groups that perform the integrating function for the system's management. These groups are made up of individuals from different departments or subunits within the overall organization (teachers, central staff, students, etc.). Their role is to learn the perspectives of all relevant parts of the system (through spaced interaction) and to bring all these conceptions to bear on plans, objectives, and the interpretation of feedback. In this way, common (superordinate) goals and decisions gradually replace subunit goals, and the organization becomes less reactive (i.e., waiting for events to happen before formulating plans) and more proactive, more open, and motivated. Integrating groups should be formed at the central level and at the individual school level. In the schools, the staff, along with student and community representatives, could perform this function: considering proposals and developing plans within the policy framework of the district. Such performance would involve special information processing or organizational training programs for principals and teachers.

The current policy-making committees in education (of which there are hundreds) rarely, if ever, achieve this level of group development and functioning. As a result, committee decisions are usually high-sounding but unworkable within the existing organizational framework.

4. Development of a "Feedback Change" System Tied to Budgeting Realities. Again, we return to a common theme running through this book. The aforementioned changes cannot occur in an informationally deprived environment. The plans that come before integrating groups should include: (a) policy framework on which the plan is based; (b) the plan; (c) specific, measurable objectives; (d) a method for evaluating the effectiveness of the plan against objective content and process criteria; and (e) cost-benefit analyses. In this way, objective feedback, when interpreted by integrating groups (and, we reiterate, that these groups are also made up of members representing *all* parts of the system—teachers and students as well as administrators, specialists, Board of Education members, etc.), produces an environment in which organizational learning and change can take root.

Research and experience demonstrate that, given conceptually mature group members, groups develop through a series of stages (Schroder et al., 1967; Schroder and Harvey, 1963; Schroder, 1971). At higher stages of conceptual development, group members are able to consider and understand educational goals from the point-of-view of the other group members and to arrive at system-level decisions and plans. To be effective, integrating groups must be of the appropriate size and design. They must be directed, in the beginning, by a specialist experienced in creating a favorable environment for group development until they arrive at a stage where true system-level decisions are generated. This procedure was demonstrated by Kennedy and Chapman in a driver licensing program and by Schroder (1970) in organizational planning for an educational system.

SOME SUGGESTED MEASURES TO ASSESS THE PROGRESS AND/OR EFFECTIVENESS OF PROCESS OBJECTIVES IN EDUCATION

Once an educational organization has determined its pedagogical objectives, it must have some way of evaluating the ongoing educative experience to detemine whether or not those objectives are being realized. In the case of process objectives in our schools, this means measuring the degree and effectiveness of process education as a consequence of various academic programs and materials, and utilizing this information in future educational planning.

Process objectives can be measured at the individual student level if tests are available that assess process learning independently from content learning. *At the school level,* progress toward process objectives can be assessed by such indices as the percentages of students receiving process and content grades and the effectiveness of process and content learning in unsupervised and supervised classroom periods. (As the educational system develops in the child a sense of intrinsic motivation, and as effective process materials become more readily available for student use, we would predict that an increasing number of students will be able to work enthusiastically and constructively with process materials in unsupervised classrooms.) We propose that a primary criteria for process education is the degree to which students engage in self-directed instruction. This is a system-level criteria reflecting the degree to which the academic environment and personnel support process learning.

Another measure of process education is the degree to which its use leads to a diminution of hostile, antischool acts by the student. This can be determined by examining the student's school absences, time spent loitering away from class (e.g., in corridors, toilets), damage to school property, and aggressive acts toward school authorities.

A measurement of the amount of resources devoted to process objectives could be assessed by how frequently process teaching was taking place in the schools. Here one might measure the number of units taught with process materials, the frequency of process tests in the classroom, the number of teachers trained in process methods, the tabulation of behavior patterns of pupils and teachers in the classroom (Vincent, 1967, 1969), resources and time devoted to self-instruction, and so on.

IMPLEMENTING PROCESS OBJECTIVES IN EDUCATION

Once an organizational structure has evolved in education that allows for process learning in the schools, efforts can be directed at implementing process objectives in the classroom. These efforts will vary, obviously, according to several factors including the specific needs of various educational districts, but they will involve the development of process materials and tests along lines already discussed; the settting up of interacting planning groups from various parts of the educational system; the development of school staffs and procedures for carrying out and measuring process objectives; initiation of in-service teacher training programs and, where possible, preservice teacher training; and the calculation of budget requirements for process programs.

In the implementation phase of the organizational program for process learning in our schools, the educational system will evolve toward assessing its effectiveness in terms of content *and* process goals; *intrinsic* as well as extrinsic controls in motivating children in the classroom. In this manner, educational institutions will increasingly provide an environment in which our children will develop the ability to exercise responsible choice, to be free, and to participate constructively with others in a changing world.

SUMMARY

In this final chapter of the book, it was proposed that developmental reforms in educational organization would have to take place *before* process goals could be realized in American schools. Two unsuccessful attempts to bring process learning to the classroom were presented to document the futility of introducing process education into a system that is not organized or ready to receive it.

Utilizing an analogy based on information-processing theory, it was argued that current content-centered educational organization functions as a unit much like a student with low information-processing skills functions as an individual. At such a level of development, it was pointed out, the various parts of the educational system—teachers, students, parents and administrators—could not interact effectively and benefit from each other's perspectives; experiences necessary for the implementation of a successful process-learning program in the schools.

Recommendations for changing the educational organization to accommodate process learning were forwarded. These recommendations, based on research findings, involved a restructuring of the educational bureaucratic structure so that teachers played a more central role in the student's development and specially selected planning committees became the major policy making force in pedagogical matters.

The chapter concluded with some recommended measures for assessing the progress and/or effectiveness of process objectives in education and some procedures for implementing process programs in the classroom.

Notes

1. The area of intelligence tests has long been a battleground with concomitant high emotions. Much confusion has existed as to what the tests actually measure, what they predict, and what they "tell" about an individual. Over the years, psychologists have constructed veritable mountains of intelligence tests, and institutions such as Educational Testing Service have developed impartial, inexpensive, and efficient procedures for mass testing on a national scale—the end result being that each tested applicant is assigned a number or percentile ranking called "intelligence." This number is then indelibly affixed to that child's record so that, forever after, everyone from the school psychologist to the first-grade teacher to the university admissions committee to the corporation interviewer can use it to judge him. It is this same number that will play a large part in determining how well the child does achieve in the school situation (Rosenthal and Jacobson, 1968). That is, it is this number that shapes what the training agent (in this case, the teacher) expects the child can do and, thus, is all the child often will do. In such a fashion, the closed loop of a self-fulfilling prophecy is initiated and "validated" or justified. It is this same number that is used, in large part, to determine who shall be admitted to many of our private elementary and secondary schools, who shall go to college and graduate school, who shall be awarded scholarships and fellowships, and who shall—as a result—have a chance for the better jobs and much of the power in the adult world.

We are not condemning IQ tests, per se. Nor are we condemning, wholesale, their usage in our schools and society. Rather, we wish to point out that such tests are only *one* definition of intelligence. That is, their greatest accuracy is in predicting how well a child *may* do in the traditional, content-oriented school situation. They indicate the child's potential ability to achieve high grades in school—grades that are based upon an evaluation of how much content the child has ingested.

Finally, it should be understood that the IQ tests themselves and the school grades against which they are validated are accurate only to the extent that: (1) the student's interest is highly aroused, (2) he has the ability to recall what he has been previously told, and (3) he can retrieve the previously memorized content at the time of the examination. To whatever degree he lacks sufficient interest or cannot retrieve the information, to that degree, his performance on the given intelligence scale or achievement test or midterm course examination will be lowered, and his intelligence quotient, percentile ranking, or course grade will be reduced.

2. In many respects the "poor scholar" is similar to Taylor's description of the high creative–low school achiever who is mistreated and often destroyed by schools but who is valuable to the culture.

3. The impact of school environments on students' behavior is more fully explicated in the 1969, volume 4 edition of *Harvard Educational Review*. Of particular interest is the article by Giancarlo de Carlo.

4. These theorists, practitioners, and others were influenced by the theorizing of William James and, broadly speaking, followed in the pedagogical tradition flowing from Comenius, Montaigne, and Rousseau.

5. As Dewey himself stated in *Experience and Education* (1938): "Because the older education imposed the knowledge, methods, and the rules of conduct of the mature person upon the young, it does not follow . . . that the knowledge and skill of the mature person has no directive value for the experience of the immature. . . . For any theory and set of practices is dogmatic which is not based upon critical examination of its own underlying principles."

6. This is what Neill also finds in his work with children at his school, Summerhill.

7. There have been a few notable exceptions in the last few years (see Cole, 1970; Cole and Sefarian, 1970; Sefarian and Cole, 1972).

8. Some efforts to establish social-studies laboratories have been stymied by financial considerations. Recently Lippitt, Fox and Schaible (1969) devised Social Science Laboratory Units that can be used in schools for relatively little cost. Such innovations increase the likelihood that process education will eventually make its way into the classroom.

9. This finding also suggests why closing the economic gap between blacks and whites can sometimes reduce prejudice. As black and white people approach equality in occupations and income, they begin to participate more frequently in equal status interaction. And once blacks and whites interact in such a manner, the chance for conceptual maturity in interpersonal relations is enhanced.

10. All such activities should be designed to ensure they are process environments that encourage process learning (as well as the acquisition of content skills). In most contemporary schools, student government is a farce and even if students are given meaningful powers, this does not guarantee that such powers will aid students in developing process ability.

Appendix A

The Inductive Teaching Program's
57 Category Fixed Program Deck for the
Community Development Exercise

1 Adornment
2 Agriculture
3 Animal husbandry
4 Armed forces, military technology and war
5 Building and construction
6 Childhood training (socialization)
7 Chemical industries
8 Clothing
9 Communication
10 Drugs and medicine
11 Economics
12 Education
13 Energy, power, light, and heat
14 Equipment in, and maintenance of, buildings
15 Family
16 Fine arts
17 Fishing and marine hunting
18 Food consumption
19 Food processing and preservation
20 Geography (physical characteristics of the island and its environment)
21 Government
22 History of the island and its inhabitants
23 Hunting and trapping
24 Ideas about nature and man
25 Interpersonal relations
26 Kinship and kin groups
27 Labor
28 Land use and land ownership
29 Language
30 Law and the execution of justice
31 Leather, textiles and fabrics
32 Life cycle: infancy, childhood, adolescence, adulthood, and old age
33 Life and death
34 Liquid consumption
35 Living standards and daily routines
36 Machines and appliances
37 Marriage
38 Mobility and social stratification
39 Narcotics, stimulants and tobacco
40 Natoma
41 Natural resources
42 Numbers and measures
43 Offenses and punishments
44 Personality characteristics of the natives
45 Physical characteristics and capabilities of the natives
46 Population movement

47 Recreation, entertainment and ceremonies
48 Religion
49 Sales promotion and corporate organization
50 Sex and reproduction
51 Sickness
52 Social problems
53 Structures (houses, etc.)
54 Tools
55 Total culture
56 Travel and transportation
57 Vital statistics: characteristics of the island population (demography)

Appendix B

A Brief Description of the
Inductive Teaching Program and the
Community Development Exercise (CODE)

COMPOSITION OF THE INDUCTIVE TEACHING PROGRAM

The Inductive Teaching Program normally consists of four interrelated, component parts.

A. The Fixed Program Deck (FPD). The Fixed Program Deck consists of any items of information about a given environment transmitted to the student without his request. Such items can take the form of informational items representative of a larger body of material the student must eventually ask questions about or categories (topics) relating to various aspects of a given environment. If such categories are supplied to the learner he may be required to utilize them in his question request, for example, assign each question he asks to the most appropriate category available. The Fixed Program Deck serves the following educational functions: (1) it assures a minimal level of familiarity with a given problem among all students; (2) it acquaints the student with the types of information that can be received.

B. The Reactive Program Deck (RPD). This program contains all the answer cards available on a given environment (problem), one or more of which is presented to the student when he asks specific questions concerning the task he is exploring. The number and type of Reactive Program Deck cards given to the learner are entirely determined by the number and type of questions the learner asks. The Reactive Program Deck gets its name from the fact that, unlike the Fixed Program Deck items that are given to the student regardless of his actions, the RPD "reacts" to students' information requests with appropriate answers. The Reactive Program Deck serves two purposes: (1) it provides the means by which students' information search can be analyzed; (2) it supplies the student with the information he needs to be able to carry out all facets of the experimental task.

C. Rule Violation Cards (RVC). Students are informed of four writing restrictions that are to be observed in composition of questions. Rule Violation Cards replace answer cards when: (1) more than one question is asked per card; (2) questions are inferential in nature (require "inferential" rather than factual answers to questions); (3) questions are longer than two sentences; (4) an answer to a question has already been received on a previous card. Rule Violation Cards serve the important function of imposing necessary restrictions on students' compositional output, ensuring necessary uniformity in the form, length, and type of questions asked.

D. No Answer Cards (NAC). Before working with the Inductive Teaching Program, students are informed that ". . . we believe that we have answered the majority of any questions that might arise, however, some information might not be available concerning your question, either because that aspect of the problem has not been studied or because we have not anticipated your question. In the case where your question cannot be answered you will receive a card stating that no information is available on the question asked."

With the advent of computers, the instructional quality of inductive training should improve dramatically. With these machines, the problem of giving the student accurate, adequate and rapid responses to all his questions can be solved. In such a system, questions can be coded and typed directly into the computer (via on-line facilities). Seconds later the appropriate answer will appear on a TV monitor in front of the child.

A BRIEF DESCRIPTION OF THE COMMUNITY DEVELOPMENT EXERCISE

In the Community Development Exercise each student was asked to imagine he was a Peace Corps volunteer who had just received his overseas assignment. His supervisor has just informed him that a mainland government in the South Pacific has requested his aid in a community development project on the island of Wabowa, some 250 miles from its coast. His assignment was to build, in a cooperative effort with the local natives, a hospital on the island. He was informed that a similar task had been attempted by missionaries three years before but that these individuals were unable to enlist native aid and the project failed. The importance of getting the hopsital built was emphasized to each individual: venereal disease was spreading rapidly on the island— killing the natives and infecting traders in the area—much to the chagrin of the mainland government. Utilizing his information search prerogatives, the student was expected to learn about the culture of the islanders he would be living with and in such a way present a tentative solution to the problem, for example, his estimation of the *best possible way* to get native approval and cooperation in building the hospital.

The major problem confronted in designing the Community Development Exercise was creating the Wabowan culture. This was accomplished by basing the Wabowan culture on the Trobriand islanders, a South Seas tribe studied extensively by Malinowski and described in his book *Argonauts of the Western Pacific* (1922). Malinowski's scholarship was instrumental in producing an adequate ITP, for by presenting a detailed, elaborate, and exacting picture of the Trobrianders, set in the larger cultural matrix of the interacting island tribes of the Trobriand archipelago, he presented a culture with enough richness to serve as a useful model for generating the necessary complexity in the Wabowan culture.

The design of the ITP for the Community Development Exercise was accomplished in two stages. In the first stage of design 1250 units of information on the Wabowan islanders were composed and placed into 57 categories. Each of the 57 categories contained between 10 and 30 pieces of information. Each item of information was expressed in a sentence between 40 and 65 characters in length. Each of these items was then reproduced 50 times, using the 1410 IBM computer, and interpreted (printed). Over 30,000 cards were prepared in this manner. These cards were used to answer the inquiries of 187 persons who generated over 10,000 questions in trying to solve the problem.

The second stage of design consisted of utilizing the 10,000 questions to improve the Fixed and Reactive Program Decks in the following ways: (1)

a new list of 57 categories for the FPD was constructed (see Appendix A), making the categories more inclusive, more understandable, and more mutually exclusive in relation to other categories. The effectiveness of the FPD was greatly enhanced by extensive utilization of the coding and categorizing techniques developed by the Human Relations Area Files (Murdock et al., 1950); (2) answers were prepared to questions that were unanswerable with the first stage Reactive Program Deck. In its final form the second stage Reactive Program Deck was more than twice the size of its first stage counterpart (2755 items) and was far more capable of answering the majority of questions asked by the testees—a requirement that is vital to the proper functioning of the Inductive Teaching Program.

For a more detailed description of the Community Development Exercise and its Inductive Teaching Program, the reader is referred to Karlins (1967).

Bibliography

Adams, H. (1961). *The education of Henry Adams: an autobiography.* Second edition (first edition, 1918). Boston: Houghton-Mifflin.

Adorno, T. W., E. Frenkel-Brunswik, D. J. Levinson, and R. N. Sanford (1950). *The authoritarian personality.* New York: Harper.

Agee, J. and W. Evans (1941). *Let us now praise famous men.* Boston: Houghton.

Allport, G. W. (1954). *The nature of prejudice.* Reading, Massachusetts: Addison-Wesley.

Anderson, H. H. (1965). On the meaning of creativity. In H. H. Anderson (editor), *Creativity in childhood and adolescence.* Palo Alto, California: Science and Behavior Books. Pp. 46–61.

Anderson, A. R. and O. K. Moore (1960). Autotelic folk models. *Sociol. Quarter., 1,* 203–216.

Architecture and education. *Harvard Education Review* (1969), *39,* No. 4.

Armitage, C. A. (1970). Information processing and system development. Princeton: Unpublished senior thesis, Princeton University.

Ashmore, R. D. (1969). Intergroup contact as a prejudice-reduction technique: an experimental examination of the shared-coping approach and four alternative explanations. Los Angeles: Unpublished doctoral dissertation, University of California at Los Angeles.

——— (1970). The problem of intergroup prejudice, and solving the problem of prejudice. In B. E. Collins (editor), *Social Psychology.* Reading, Massachusetts: Addison-Wesley. Pp. 247–339.

Ausubel, D. P. (1965). In defense of verbal learning. In R. C. Anderson and D. P. Ausubel (editors), *Readings in the psychology of cognition.* New York: Holt, Rinehart & Winston. Pp. 87–102.

——— (1966). Meaningful reception learning and the acquisition of concepts. In H. Klausmeier and C. W. Harris (editors), *Analyses of concept learning.* New York: Academic Press. Pp. 157–175.

Berlyne, D. E. (1965). *Structure and direction of thinking.* New York: John Wiley.

Biber, B. (1967). A learning-teaching paradigm integrating intellectual and affective processes. In E. M. Bower and W. G. Hollister (editors), *Behavioral science frontiers in education.* New York: John Wiley. P. 131.

Biggs, J. B. (1968). *Information and human learning.* Melbourne, Australia: Cassell.

Bruner, J. S. (1960). *The process of education.* Cambridge: Harvard University Press.

——— (1966). *Toward a theory of instruction.* Cambridge: Harvard University Press.

Bruner, J. S., J. J. Goodnow, and G. A. Austin (1956). *A study of thinking.* New York: John Wiley.

Burnstein, E. and A. V. McCree (1962). Some effects of shared threat and prejudice in racially mixed groups. *J. abnom. soc. Psychol., 64,* 257–263.

Carrington, J. H. (1970). Personal communication.

Charlesworth, W. R. (1964). Instigation and maintenance of curiosity behavior as a function of surprise versus novel and familiar stimuli. *Child Dev., 35,* 1169–1186.

Coffman, T. L. (1967). Personality structure, involvement, and the consequences of taking a stand. Princeton: Unpublished doctoral dissertation, Princeton University.

Cole, H. P. (1970). *Process education: an emerging rational position.* Syracuse, New York: Eastern Regional Institute for Education.

Cole, H. P. and A. Sefarian (1970). Analysis of process curricula. In *Research into process curricula.* Syracuse, New York: Eastern Regional Institute for Education.

Crouse, B., M. Karlins, and H. M. Schroder (1968). Conceptual complexity and marital happiness. *J. Marriage & Family, 30,* 643–646.

Dewey, J. (1891). *My pedagogic creed.* Boston: Heath.

——— (1910). *How we think.* Boston: Heath.

Driver, M. J. (1962). Conceptual structure and group processes in an internation simulation. Part one: The perception of simulated nations. *Educational Testing Service Research Bulletin,* RB 62–15.

Erikson, E. (1950). *Childhood and society.* New York: Norton. P. 210.

Fesbach, S. and R. Singer (1957). The effects of personal and shared threats upon social prejudice. *J. abnorm. soc. Psychol., 54,* 411–416.
Friedenberg, E. (1967). *Coming of age in America.* New York: Vantage Books.
Fromm, E. (1941). *Escape from freedom.* New York: Holt, Rinehart & Winston.

Gagné, R. M. (1965). *The conditions of learning.* New York: Holt, Rinehart & Winston.
——— (1966). Varieties of learning and the concept of discovery. In L. S. Shulman and E. R. Kreisler (editors), *Learning by discovery.* Chicago: Rand McNally.
——— (1967). *Learning and individual differences.* Columbus, Ohio: Charles E. Merrill.
Gardiner, G. S. (1971). Complexity training and prejudice reduction. Princeton: Unpublished doctoral dissertation, Princeton University.
Gardner, J. W. (1961). *Excellence—Can we be equal and excellent too?* New York: Harper & Row.
Goodlad, J. I. (1969). The schools vs. education. *Saturday Review, 52(16),* 59:61, 80–82.
Guilford, J. P. (1965). Three faces of intellect. In R. P. Anderson and D. P. Ausubel (editors), *Readings in the psychology of cognition.* New York: Holt, Rinehart & Winston. Pp. 194–214.
——— (1965b). The structure of intellect. *Psychol. Bull., 53,* 267–293.
——— (1967). *The nature of human intelligence.* New York: McGraw-Hill.

Hall, G. S. (1914). Aspects of child life and education (T. L. Smith, editor). Boston: Ginn & Co.
Harris, B. M. (1962). Ten myths that have led education astray. *The Nation's Schools,* April.
Havelock, R. G. (1969). Planning for innovation through dissemination and utilization of knowledge. Ann Arbor, Michigan: Center for Research on Utilization of Scientific Knowledge. As cited in H. P. Cole (1970), *Process education: an emerging rational position.* Syracuse, New York: Eastern Regional Institute for Education.
——— (1970). A guide to innovation in education. As cited in H. P. Cole (1970), *Process education: an emerging rational position.* Syracuse, New York: Eastern Regional Institute for Education.
Haythorne, W. (1953). The influence of individual members on the characteristics of small groups. *J. abnorm. soc. Psychol., 48,* 276–284.
Haythorne, W., A. Couch, D. Harfner, P. Longham, and L. F. Carter (1956a). The behavior of authoritarian and egalitarian personalities in groups. *Human Relat., 9,* 57–74.

———— (1956b). The effects of varying combinations of authoritarian and egalitarian leaders and followers. *J. abnorm. soc. Psychol., 53,* 210–219.

Hebb, D. O. (1949). *The organization of behavior; a neuropsychological theory.* New York: John Wiley.

Hendrick, I. (1943). The discussion of the "instinct to master." *Psychoanalytic Quart., 12,* 561–565.

Hunt, D. E. (1966). A conceptual systems change model and its application to education. In O. J. Harvey (editor), *Experience, structure and adaptability.* New York: Springer.

———— (1970). Matching models and moral training. In C. Beck, B. Crittendon, and E. V. Sullivan, (editors), *Moral education.* Toronto, Canada: University of Toronto Press.

———— (1971). *Matching models in education.* Toronto: Ontario Institute for Studies in Education.

Hunt, J. McV. (1961). *Intelligence and experience.* New York: Ronald Press.

———— (1966). Toward a theory of guided learning in development. In R. H. Ojemann and K. Pritchett (editors), *Giving emphasis to guided learning.* Cleveland: Educational Research Council.

———— (1969). Has compensatory education failed? Has it been attempted? *Harvard Ed. Review,* Spring, *39* (2), 278–300.

———— (1971a). Intrinsic motivation: information and circumstances. In H. M. Schroder and P. Suedfeld (editors), *Personality: theory and information processing.* New York: Ronald Press. Pp. 85–130.

———— (1971b). Intrinsic motivation and psychological development. In H. M. Schroder and P. Suedfeld (editors), *Personality theory and information processing.* New York: Ronald Press. Pp. 131–177.

Jensen, A. R. (1969). How much can we boost IQ and scholastic achievement? *Harvard Ed. Review,* Winter, *39* (1), 1–123.

Karlins, M. (1967). Conceptual complexity and remote-associate proficiency as creativity variables in a complex problem-solving task. *J. Person. Soc. Psychol., 6,* 264–278.

———— (1968a). Examining creativity with the Inductive Teaching Program. *J. Special Ed., 2,* 167–176.

———— (1968b). Some empirical support for an exploration stage in the creative process. *J. Creative Behavior, 2,* 256–262.

Karlins, M., T. Coffman, H. Lamm, and H. M. Schroder (1967a). The effect of conceptual complexity on information search in a complex problem-solving task. *Psychon. Sci., 7,* 137–138.

Karlins, M., R. Lee, and H. M. Schroder (1967b). Creativity and information search in a problem-solving context. *Psychon. Sci., 8,* 165–166.

Karlins, M. and H. Lamm. (1967c). Information search as a function of conceptual structure in a complex problem-solving task. *J. Person. soc. Psychol., 5,* 456–459.

Kennedy, J. L. (1962). The systems approach: organizational development. *Hum. Factors, 4,* 25–52.

Kilpatrick, W. H. (1925). *Foundations of method.* New York: New American Library.

Lee, R. E., III (1968). Dispositional and induced information processing structures. Princeton: Unpublished doctoral dissertation. Princeton University.

Likert, R. (1961). *New patterns of management.* New York: McGraw-Hill.

———— (1967). *The human organization: its management and value.* New York: McGraw-Hill.

Lippitt, R. (1964). Roles and processes in curriculum development and change. In *Strategy for curriculum change.* Washington, D.C.: Association for Supervision and Curriculum Development.

Lippitt, R., R. Fox, and L. Schaible (1969). *The teacher's role in social science investigation.* Chicago: Science Research Associates.

Malinowski, B. (1922). *Argonauts of the western world.* New York: Dunston.

Mann, J. H. (1959). The effect of inter-racial contact on sociometric choices and perceptions. *J. Soc. Psychol, 50,* 143–152.

Maslow, A. H. (1962). *Toward a psychology of being.* Second edition (first edition, 1960). Princeton: Van Nostrand.

———— (1970). *Motivation and personality.* Second edition (first edition, 1954). New York: Harper & Row.

McLachlan, J. F. and D. E. Hunt (in press). Differential effects of discovery learning as a function of student's conceptual level. *Canadian J. Behavior. Sci.*

Miles, M. B. (editor) (1967). *Innovation in education.* New York: Teachers College Press.

Miller, G. (1956). The magical number seven, plus or minus two: some limits on our capacity for processing information. *Psychol. Rev., 63,* 81–97.

Moore, O. K. and A. R. Anderson (1967). The responsive environments project. In R. D. Hess and R. M. Bear (editors), *Early education: current theory, research and practice.* Chicago: Aldine Publishing Co.

Neill, A. S. (1960). *Summerhill: a radical approach to child rearing.* New York: Hart Publishing Co.

Phares, J. O., G. S. Gardiner, and H. M. Schroder (1971). *Creativity/complexity in the social studies.* An evaluation of the social studies curriculum, grades four through six, EdCom Systems, Inc., Princeton, New Jersey.

Phares, J. O. and H. M. Schroder (1969). *A structural scoring manual for the Paragraph Completion Test.* Unpublished manuscript, Princeton University.

Piaget, J. (1952). *The origins of intelligence in children.* Second edition (first edition, 1936). New York: International Universities Press.

———— (1963). *The psychology of intelligence.* Second edition (first edition, 1947). Paterson, New Jersey: Littlefield, Adams & Co.

Postman, N. and C. Weingartner (1969). *Teaching as a subversive activity.* New York: Delacorte Press.

Razik, T. A. (1967). Psychometric measurement of creativity. In R. Mooney and T. Razik (editors), *Explorations in creativity.* New York: Harper & Row. P. 303.

Rimoldi, H., J. Haley, H. Fogliatto, and J. Erdmann (1963). A program for the study of thinking. ONR Technical Report, University of Loyola Psychometric Laboratory.

Roethlisberger, F. J. (1956). *Management and morale.* Cambridge: Harvard University Press.

Rogers, C. R. (1951). *Client-centered therapy.* Boston: Houghton-Mifflin.

——— (1961). *On becoming a person: a therapist's view of psychotherapy.* Boston: Houghton-Mifflin.

——— (1969). *Freedom to learn.* Columbus, Ohio: Charles E. Merrill.

Rosenthal, R. and L. Jacobson (1968). *Pygmalion in the classroom.* New York: Holt, Rinehart & Winston.

Schmuck, R. A. (1968). Helping teachers improve classroom group processes. *J. applied Behavior. Sci., 20,* 204–214.

Schroder, H. M. (1970). *The measurement and development of management information systems.* Paper read at the International Conference on Management Information Systems, Köln, Germany.

——— (1971a). Conceptual composition and personality organization. In H. M. Schroder and P. Suedfeld (editors), *Personality theory and information processing.* New York: Ronald Press. Pp. 240–275.

——— (1971b). A process environment for inter-disciplinary programs at the university level. Unpublished manuscript. Southern Illinois University.

Schroder, H. M., M. J. Driver, and S. Streufert (1967). *Human information processing.* New York: Holt, Rinehart & Winston.

Schroder, H. M. and O. J. Harvey (1963). Conceptual organization and group structure. In O. J. Harvey (editor), *Motivation and social interaction: cognitive determinants.* New York: Ronald Press. Pp. 134–166.

Sefarian, R. and H. P. Cole (in press). *Encounters in thinking: a compendium of curricula for process education.* Syracuse: Creative Education Foundation.

Senders, V. (1958). *Measurement and statistics.* New York: Oxford University Press.

Sherif, M. (1958). Superordinate goals in the reduction of inter-group conflict. *Amer. J. Sociol, 63,* 349–363.

Sherif, M. and C. Sherif (1953). *Groups in harmony and tension; an integration of studies on inter-group relations.* New York: Harper.

Silberman, C. E. (1970). *Crisis in the classroom.* New York: Random House.

Singer, D. (1969). The impact of interracial classroom exposure on the social attitudes of fifth grade children. Cited in J. Harding, B. Kutner, H. Proshansky, and I. Cheis, "Prejudice and ethnic relations." In G. Lindzey and E. Aronson (editors), *Handbook of social psychology*, (second edition), Vol. 5, Reading, Massachusetts: Addison-Wesley.

Stager, D. P. (1966). Conceptual level as a composition variable in small group decision making. *J. Person, soc. Psychol, 4,* 100–103.

Streufert, S. and M. J. Driver (1966). Conceptual structure, information load and conceptual complexity. *Psychon. Sci., 3,* 249–250.

Streufert, S. (1962). Attitude generalization in social triads as a function of personality structure and availability of social support. Princeton: ONR Technical Report.

———— (1966). Conceptual structure, communicator importance, and interpersonal attitudes toward deviant and conforming group members. *J. Person. soc. Psychol., 4,* 100–103.

Streufert, S. and H. M. Schroder (1965). Conceptual structure, environmental complexity and task performance. *J. exp. res. Person., 1,* 132–137.

Suchman, R. J. (1961). Inquiry training: building skills for autonomous discovery. *Merrill-Palmer Quart., 7,* 147–169.

Tomkins, S. S. (1963). The right and the left: a basic dimension of ideology and personality. In R. W. White (editor), *The Study of lives.* New York: Atherton Press. Pp. 338–411.

Tonlinson, T. D. and D. E. Hunt (1971). *Differential effects of rule-example order as a function of learner conceptual level. Canadian J. Behavior. Sci., 3,* 237–245.

Torrance, E. P. (1968). A longitudinal examination of the fourth grade slump in creativity. *The Gifted Child Quart., 12* (4), 195–199.

Tuckman, B. W. (1964). Personality structure, group composition, and group functioning. *Sociometry, 27,* 469–487.

Vincent, W. S. (1967). Indicators of quality. New York: Teachers College, Columbia University. *IAR-Research Bulletin, 12,* 1–5.

———— (1969) (editor). *Signs of good teaching.* New York: Columbia University Press.

Wallach, M. and N. Kogan. (1965). *Modes of thinking in young children.* New York: Holt, Rinehart & Winston.

White, R. W. (1959). Motivation reconsidered: the concept of competence. *Psychol. Rev., 66,* 297–333.

———— (1960). Competence and psychosexual stages of development. *Nebraska Symposium on Motivation, 8,* 96–141.

Williams, R. M. (1964). *Strangers next door: ethnic relations in American communities.* Englewood Cliffs, New Jersey: Prentice-Hall.

FURTHER READINGS

Anderson, C. C. (1968). Galbraith, technology, and education. *Alberta Jrl. Ed. Research, XIV,* Mar., 5–13.

Anderson, H. H. (1965). On the meaning of creativity. In H. H. Anderson (editor), *Creativity in childhood and adolescence.* Palo Alto, California: Science & Behavior Books.

Anderson, R. C. and D. P. Ausubel (1966). *Readings in the psychology of cognition.* New York: Holt, Rinehart & Winston.

Bereiter, C. and S. Engelmann (1966). *Teaching disadvantaged children in the pre-school.* Englewood Cliffs, New Jersey: Prentice-Hall.

Bennix, W. G. (1966). *Changing organizations.* New York: McGraw-Hill.

Bennix, W. G., and P. E. Slater (1968). *The temporary society.* New York: Harper & Row.

Berkowitz, L. (1964). *The development of motives and values in the child.* New York: Basic Books.

Bruner, J. S. (1957). Going beyond the information given. In J. S. Bruner, E. Brunswik, L. Festinger, F. Heider, K. Muenzinger, C. E. Osgood, and D. Rapaport, *Contemporary approaches to cognition.* A symposium held at the University of Colorado. Cambridge: Harvard University Press.

——— (1969). *On knowing: essays for the left hand.* New York: Atheneum.

——— (1970). The skill of relevance or the relevance of skills. *Sat. Review, 53,* (14), 66–68, 78–79.

Bruner, J. S. and P. B. Dow (1967). *Man: a course of study, a description of an elementary social studies curriculum.* Cambridge: Educational Development Center.

Bruner, J. S., R. R. Olver, P. M. Greenfield *et. al.* (1966). *Studies in cognitive growth.* New York: John Wiley.

Charters, W. W. (1963). The social background of teaching. In N. L. Gage (editor), *Handbook of research in teaching.* Chicago: Rand McNally.

Coleman, J. S. *et. al.* (1966). *Equality of educational opportunity.* U.S. Department of Health, Education and Welfare.

Cronbach, L. J. (1967). How can instruction be adapted to individual differences? In R. M. Gagné (editor), *Learning and individual differences.* Columbus, Ohio: Charles E. Merrill.

Fenton, E. (1966). *Teaching the new social studies in secondary schools— an inductive approach.* New York: Holt, Rinehart & Winston.

Furth, H. G. (1970). *Piaget for teachers.* Englewood Cliffs, New Jersey: Prentice-Hall.

Gagné, R. M. (1968). Contributions to human development. *Psychol. Rev., 75(3),* 177–191.

Griffith, W. (1971). A daring educational experience—the one-room school-house. *New York Times Magazine,* May 30, 1971.

Guilford, J. P. (1950). Creativity. *American Psychol., 4,* 444–445.

——— (1965). A psychometric approach to creativity. In H. H. Anderson (editor), *Creativity in childhood and adolescence.* Palo Alto, California: Science and Behavior Books.

——— (1967). Creativity: yesterday, today, and tomorrow? *J. Creat. Behavior, 1,* 3–14.

Inhelder, B. and J. Piaget (1958). *The growth of logical thinking from child-hood to adolescence.* New York: Basic Books.

Kelly, G. A. (1955). *The psychology of personal constructs. Vol. 1. A theory of personality.* New York: Norton.

Kohl, H. (1967). *Thirty six children.* New York: New American Library.

——— (1969). *The open classroom.* New York: Vintage Books.

Kohlberg, L. (1963). Moral development and identification. In H. W. Stevenson (editor), *Yearbook of the National Society for the Study of Education. Part 1: Child psychology.* Chicago: University of Chicago Press. Pp. 277–332.

——— (1964). Development of moral character and moral ideology. In M. L. Hoffman and L. W. Hoffman (editors), *Review of child development research.* New York: Russell Sage Foundation.

Kozol, J. (1967). *Death at an early age.* Boston: Little Brown.

Lewin, K. (1935). *The dynamic theory of personality.* First edition. New York: McGraw-Hill.

Maslow, A. H. (1956). Self-actualizing people. In C. E. Moustakas (editor), *The self: explorations in personal growth.* New York: Harper. Pp. 160–194.

——— (1962). Some basic propositions of a growth and self-actualization psychology. In A. W. Coombs (editor), *Perceiving, behaving, becoming. Yearbook, 1962.* Washington, D.C.: Association for Supervision and Curriculum Development.

McClelland, D. C. *et. al.* (1953). *The achievement motive.* New York: Appleton-Century-Crofts.

Noah, H. J. (1970). Education needs rational decision making. *Teachers College Record, 72,* (2), 187–200.

Parnes, S. J. (1963). Education and creativity. *Teachers College Record, 64,* (4), 331–339.

Piaget, J. (1932). *The moral judgment of the child.* New York: Harcourt Brace.

——— (1951). *Play, dreams and imitation in childhood.* New York: Norton.

Rogers, C. R. (1967). The facilitation of significant learning. In L. Siegel (editor), *Instruction: some contemporary viewpoints.* San Francisco: Chandler. Pp. 172–182.

Rokeach, M. (1960). *The open and closed mind.* New York: Basic Books.

Schneir, W. and M. Schneir (1971). The joy of learning—in the open classroom. *New York Times Magazine,* April 4, 1971.

Shulman, L. S. and E. R. Kreisler (editors) (1966). *Learning by discovery: a critical appraisal.* Chicago: Rand McNally.

Skinner, B. F. (1968). *The technology of teaching.* New York: Appleton-Century-Crofts.

Summerhill: For and Against (1970). New York: Hart.

Taylor, C. W. and F. E. Williams (1966). *Instructional media and creativity,* The proceedings of the 6th Utah Creativity Research Conference. New York: John Wiley.

Triandis, H. C. (1964). Cultural influences upon cognitive processes. In L. Berkowitz (editor), *Advances in experimental social psychology.* New York: Academic Press.

Walker, W. J. (1969). Teacher personality in creative school environments. *J. ed. Research,* February, 1969.

Whitehead, A. N. (1929). The aims of education. New York: New American Library.

Author Index

Hendrick, I., 45
Hollister, W. G., 8
Hunt, David E., 43, 45, 46, 74, 88
Hunt, J. McV., 5

Jacobson, L., 104
James, William, 104
Jensen, A. R., 43

Karlins, M., 5, 28, 37, 38, 67, 68, 82, 98, 114
Kennedy, J. L., 98, 100
Kilpatrick, W. H., 18
Kogan, N., 37
Kohlberg, L., 88

Lamm, H., 67
Lee, R. E., III, 37, 43, 81
Likert, R., 98
Lippitt, R., 59, 95, 105

Malinowski, B., 113
Mann, J. H., 85
Maslow, A. H., 18, 79
Miles, M. B., 98
Miller, G., 34
Montaigne, 104
Mooney, R., 20
Moore, Omar K., 5, 65, 66, 73, 74

Neill, A. S., 65, 71, 105

Phares, J. O., 41, 80, 98
Piaget, J., 5, 24, 63
Postman, N., 10, 16

Razik, T. A., 20
Rimoldi, H., 42
Roethlisberger, F. J., 98
Rogers, Carl R., 18, 62, 76
Rosenthal, R., 104
Rousseau, J., 104

Schaible, L., 59, 105
Schmuck, R. A., 98
Schroder, H. M., 5, 28, 35, 37, 41, 59, 67, 69, 80, 81, 82, 98, 100
Sefarian, A., 105
Sefarian, R., 85, 105
Sherif, C., 85, 86
Sherif, M., 85, 86
Silberman, C. E., 59
Singer, R., 85
Skinner, B. F., 3
Stager, D. P., 81, 82, 98
Streufert, S., 28, 35, 67, 80, 81, 98
Suchman, R. J., 68

Taylor, C. W., 104
Tomkins, S. S., 84
Tonlinson, T. D., 74
Torrance, E. P., 1, 16, 54
Tuckman, B. W., 82, 98

Vincent, W. S., 101

Wallach, M., 37
Weingartner, C., 10, 16
White, R. W., 45
Williams, R. M., 85

Subject Index

intrinsic motivation and, 44—46, 49, 56, 59

results of, 44—48

school policy and, 71—72, 94—101

in social sciences, 71, 105

teacher ability and, 29—35, 70—71, 95

teacher role in, 96, 97, 98—99

tests for, 36—42, 80—81, 86—88, 100—101

see also Educational environment; Information-processing ability

Programmed learning, 11, 66

Progressive education, *see* Permissive education systems

Reading, teaching of, 14—15

Reception learning, 60; *see also* Content learning

Reinforcement, learning by, 3, 11

"Sesame Street," 10

Small-group interaction, for process learning, 63—64

Social development, 77—89

information-processing ability and, 80—83

prejudice potential, 83—85

prejudice reduction and, 85—88

stress situations and, 82, 84

Social sciences, process learning in, 71, 105

Student government, 105

Student interaction, 63—64

Summerhill, 65

'Talking typewriter," in process learning, 65—66

Teacher, in content-learning system, 11, 12, 26

in process-learning system, 26, 29—35, 70—71, 96, 97, 98—99

role of, 10—11

Teaching assistants, in process learning, 97

Technological change, 1—2, 3—4

social problems caused by, 1—2

Tests, of information-processing ability, 36—42, 80—81, 86—88

Traditional methods, *see* Content learning

DATE DUE			
DE 2			
MY 17 7			
June 7			

Schroder   149272